THE FRENCH SCHOOL OF SPIRITUALITY & JOHN BAPTIST DE LA SALLE

Laurence Rondinet

Legal department, Public Relations

Service juridique et des relations extérieures

Foreign rights : acquisitions, sales - Second/Subsidiary and reproduction rights

Déléguée aux droits étrangers, ventes et acquisitions - Droits annexes et de reproduction

Les Éditions du Cerf

24, rue des Tanneries

75013 Paris

France

Ligne directe / My Direct line : 00 33 1 80 05 36 21

Fax : 00 33 1 80 05 36 10

Cover/Interior Design and Composition by Agápe Design Studios, Winona, MN. Published by the Institute of Lasallian Studies of Saint Mary's University of Minnesota, Winona, MN 55987.

Cover Image: Used by permission. Charles Le Brun, Pentecost, 1665-68, Oil on wood. Paris, Séminaire Saint Sulpice, © Society of Saint Sulpice.

Printed in the United States of America

ISBN: 978-0-9886583-2-5

THE FRENCH SCHOOL OF SPIRITUALITY & JOHN BAPTIST DE LA SALLE

YVES KRUMENACKER

Translated by Allen Geppert, FSC

Foreword by Gerard Rummery, FSC

Edited with Introduction and Bibliography
by William Mann, FSC

CONTENTS

FOREWORD

By Gerard Rummery, FSC

In the century following the Protestant Reformation that had shattered the religious unity of Europe, the Catholic Church's priority was to implement the Catholic reform decided by the Council of Trent (1545-1563). One important aspect of this was to insist that priests should not only have studied theology, but more importantly should be trained and "formed" in seminaries to lead a deep, spiritual life.

In implementing this vision in seventeenth-century France, there emerged a number of theologians and spiritual writers, loosely referred to historically as "the French School of Spirituality." This was no formally organized group but rather contemporaries or near-contemporaries such as Cardinal Pierre de Bérulle who was the founder of the Oratory in France, Charles de Condren who became the Superior General of the Oratory, Jean Eudes who was originally a member of the Oratory before founding a society of priests as well as a congregation of women, and Jean-Jacques Olier who with two companions founded the Society of Saint-Sulpice.

The influence of these men on one another is evident through their common insistence on the goodness of God, the Spirit of Jesus, the Church as the Body of Christ, the emphasis on the holiness needed by priests, and the role of Mary as Mother of Jesus through the mystery of the Incarnation.

These themes, found in the life, actions, and writings of De La Salle, can be attributed to his two years from 18 to 20 years of age in the Seminary of Saint-Sulpice in Paris.

Contemporary writers such as Raymond Deville and Yves Krumenacker, therefore, see De La Salle's life and work in founding the Brothers of the Christian Schools as one of the practical fruits of the French School of Spirituality.

INTRODUCTION

By William Mann, FSC

A quite remarkable study of seventeenth-century spirituality in France was published in 1999. Yves Krumenacker's *L'école française de spiritualité: Des mystiques, des fondateurs, des courants et leurs interprètes*[1] examines the French or Bérullian School of Spirituality and, for our purposes, situates John Baptist de La Salle within the context of this "age of spiritual grandeur." Unfortunately, Krumenacker's work still remains relatively unknown to English-speaking audiences; but hopefully its 660-pages will someday be translated into English. However, we are pleased with this book to make a small portion – and this mainly concerned with De La Salle – available for your study and consideration.

It is not my intention to imply by this current publication that John Baptist de La Salle was, strictly speaking, a member of the French School of Spirituality. However, the spiritual currents of seventeenth-century France certainly influenced his teaching and writing. How could a well-educated person engaged in the ecclesial affairs and the educational stirrings of his age not have been influenced by what was going on around him?

My interest in this topic dates back to the winter of 1983 when I had the opportunity to participate in a five-month renewal session at the Centro Internazionale Lasalliano (CIL) in Rome. Under the direction of Brother Gerard Rummery and instructed by Brothers Maurice-Auguste Hermans, Miguel Campos, Jean Pungier, and Jacques-Didier Piveteau, the spiritual vision of De La Salle as he was coming to grips with the stirrings and realities of his time came alive for me in an unforeseen or previously unimagined way.

My ongoing study of the Founder and my reading about seventeenth-century French history and spirituality have convinced me that De La Salle was, no matter how inspired and brilliant, truly a man of his times. And the readings that I have done about the spiritual writers and the spirituality of this period have shed light, in particular, on De La Salle's *Explanation of the Method of Interior Prayer* and *Meditations.*

Key authors writing about De La Salle assert his uniqueness and caution against an over-simplified identification of the Founder with the French or Bérullian School.

Brother Michel Sauvage, in his 1990 conference entitled "The Gospel Journey of John Baptist de La Salle,"[2] comments on the originality and eclecticism of De La Salle's spiritual doctrine. He notes that:

> several historians see in John Baptist de La Salle a good witness to the many spiritual movements in the France of the seventeenth century. These are so varied as to defy categorization into schools or types. Like most of the spiritual authors of his day, De La Salle saw in Sacred Scripture the basis for the spiritual life of the Christian. Above all, he set himself in the mainstream of the Catholic Counter-Reformation and so was animated by an enthusiasm for spiritual renewal and missionary zeal. His spiritual doctrine is marked by the Christocentricism of the school of Bérulle, along with its devotion to the Word Incarnate and its identification with the "mysteries" that doctrine implies – adherence to the person of Christ, an effort to conform oneself to

> Christ and to the mind of Christ, including above all, renouncement and abnegation of self.[3]

Jesuit Father André Rayez, in his 1955 essay entitled "The Spirituality of Self-Abandonment: Saint John Baptist de La Salle,"[4] while asserting that De La Salle was "one of the best representatives of the spiritual movement of self-abandonment in the seventeenth and eighteenth centuries,"[5] notes that De La Salle:

> drew his spiritual sustenance from many varied sources. He moved freely from Olier to the Carmelite Brother Lawrence of the Resurrection, from Saint Francis de Sales to Bernières, from Saint Teresa [of Avila] to Rancé, from the Jesuit Busée to Buevelet, the disciple of Bourdoise, or yet again, from Tronson to the Minim Barré, from the Capuchin Jean-François de Reims to Canon Roland, from Maurist Claude Bretagne to the Archdeacon Boudon.[6]

In another essay entitled "Lasallian Studies in the Mid-Twentieth Century,"[7] Rayez asserts in 1952 that:

> it is much less from the leaders than from the disciples that De La Salle came to know and to imbibe the Bérullian doctrine, and this doctrine is not the whole story of his spirituality.[8]

Rayez spends some time in this 1952 essay considering two writings of De La Salle,

> *Collection of Various Short Treatises*, which is for the greater part made up of borrowed passages and summaries, and *Explanation of the Method of Interior Prayer*, which is more original and more personal and in which various influences can be detected.[9]

In so doing, he notes the influence of such authors as Canon Nicolas Roland, Jean-Jacques Olier, Ignatius of Loyola, the Jesuits (Jerome Nadal, Antoine Vatier, Jean Crasset, Jean-Joseph Surin, Jean Busée, and Jean-Baptiste Saint-Jure), Louis Tronson, Jean de Bernières and the spirit of Jean de Saint-Samson and Benôit de Canfield, Jean-François de Reims, and Henri-Marie Boudon.[10]

Brother Maurice-Auguste Hermans, in a 1981 conference entitled "Some Spiritual Currents Which Could Have Influenced De La Salle,"[11] states that:

> as is the case with very many spiritual writers, De La Salle is not simply a member of a school. He is open and welcoming to the writings of the great and modern spiritual writers. He is indebted also to the "descendants" of these writers and to authors of less importance. At a time when feelings were easily aroused between partisans and opponents of "rigorism," quietism, or simply of devotion, De La Salle succeeded in avoiding these struggles. As a consequence, he attracts less attention from researchers.[12]

Brother Miguel Campos, in his brilliant 1975 "Introduction" to the *Meditations for the Time of Retreat,*[13] notes that although the literary sources of the retreat meditations "have not been systematically studied," it:

> is nonetheless certain that Saint de La Salle was influenced by the concerns, the ideas, and the experience of the persons of his time who were engaged in the reform of schools, and especially by those who were involved in the training of teachers.[14]

He cites Institute historian Georges Rigualt as writing in 1937 about these retreat meditations that:

> this book which in several passages clearly reflects the teachings of the *Escole Paroissiale* [of Jacques de Batencour], the *Remonstrances* of Charles Demia, the *Avis* of Nicolas Roland, and the *Maximes* of Father Barré. But the teachings are broadened by all the profound and powerful dimensions of the doctrine of the Apostle Paul.[15]

Many other authors in writing about seventeenth-century spirituality and the French or Bérullian School assert its influence, either direct or indirect, on the writings of De La Salle.

Interaction with Raymond Deville at a conference I was fortunate to attend in 1989[16] heightened my awareness of this fact. [Around the same time I was also living in community in Rome with Brother Jean-Guy Rodrigue, whose 1988 study[17] of the sources of De La Salle's meditations for feast days had just been published; and this also sparked my interest.] Reading Deville's 1994 book [1987 in French] entitled *The French School of Spirituality* only reinforced my awareness of this influence. "Among the many heirs to the Bérulle School," he writes, "there are two who merit special attention: Saint John-Baptist de La Salle (1651-1719) and Saint Louis-Marie Grignion de Montfort (1673-1716). Indeed the apostolic commitments and the spiritual doctrine of these two holy men follow the tradition of the founders of the French School. Moreover, both were formed at Saint-Sulpice Seminary and were influenced in a decisive way by their directors, Louis Tronson (1622-1700) and François Leschassier (1641-1725)."[18]

Additionally, Yves Krumenacker's 1999 book entitled *The French School of Spirituality: Mystics, Founders, Movements, and Their Interpreters,* also, asserts when writing of De La Salle: "This educator of poor children ... was also very much influenced by the spirituality of Bérulle."[19]

Finally, *an annotated bibliography* is included at the conclusion of this book since it is my experience that the study of the ideas and spiritual currents of seventeenth-century writers is most helpful in deepening one's appreciation of the life, teachings, and writings of John Baptist de La Salle. It is hoped that the bibliography will encourage you to read one or other of these writings (or more) and so provide you with a broader sense of the currents of seventeenth-century French spirituality and especially of the French School of Spirituality, which I believe is one way of situating and understanding the writings of John Baptist de La Salle in a larger context.

THE FRENCH SCHOOL OF SPIRITUALITY & JOHN BAPTIST DE LA SALLE

By Yves Krumenacker

OVERVIEW

The expression the "French School of Spirituality" appears only in 1873. It is popularized by the Abbé Brémond,[20] who gave this name to the movement born of Pierre de Bérulle (1575-1629). This movement is a composite, as is pointed out in this book, which is the result of a research seminar at the faculty of theology at Lyons.

A more thorough examination of the thinking of Bérulle, followed by that of his disciples and successors – Condren, Bourgoing, the French Carmelites, Vincent de Paul, Louise de Marillac, Olier, Saint-Cyran, Jean Eudes – makes it possible to identify the major aspects of a spirituality characterized by the acute awareness of the smallness of man and the greatness of God, by the importance of the Incarnation, by a sense of the Church and of the role of the priest, and by the need of apostolic commitment in the service of the "reformation of the people."

From the middle of the 17th century, this spirit tended to disappear because of a number of factors: an increase in absolutism, a rejection of mysticism, the Jansenist quarrel, the transformation of missions, the training of "good priests." Some aspects of the Bérulle movement continue to exist in Boudon, Démia, John Baptist de La Salle, Grignion de Montfort, and the first Priests of the Foreign Missions.

It was only in the 19th century, in a very different context, that the foundations of this spirituality were gradually re-discovered, to the extent that numerous congregations today can claim to descend from this movement.[21]

FRENCH SCHOOL OR BÉRULLIANISM?[22]

The spirituality of Bérulle is not centered on a rigorous method, but emphasizes broad doctrinal and mystical views, which lend themselves to a variety of very different nuances in those who find their inspiration in them.[23]

Characteristics of the School

By what criteria can we define this "school"? Raymond Deville suggests five.[24] First of all, "a certain degree of emphasis and insistence on this or that aspect of the Christian faith or life in the spirit." In the case we are studying, the points emphasized are a sense of transcendence and of the holiness of God, of intimate union with the life of Jesus, of abandonment to his Spirit, of devotion to Mary, Queen of All, and of the greatness of the priesthood. The second criterion is "a certain manner of praying and a certain approach to the mission." For Bérulle and his disciples, Christian prayer is wholly centered on Jesus and his mysteries, whether it is the prayer of the Church or personal meditation [*oraison*]. The aim of the mission is to bring to birth "the Life and the Kingdom of Jesus in Christian souls" – according to the title of a book by Jean Eudes – and to promote interior religion. Thirdly, there are "some pedagogical elements." We pick out a few: the importance given to liturgical feasts, the methods of interior prayer [*oraison*], meditation on the Bible, spiritual direction, vows of servitude. Deville then suggests a study of the "favorite biblical texts." In this case, the preferred texts are the Gospel of Saint John and the Epistles of Saint Paul. One could complement this criterion, by considering also favorite authors. Here we find that Saint Augustine, the Greek Fathers, and the mystics have been much meditated on by all the spiritual writers we have studied. Finally, "schools of spirituality are rooted in a very strong spiritual experience," an experience which can be complex. For Bérulle, as for his disciples, one could probably characterize it by the violence of the contradiction between the greatness of God, the religious ignorance of the common people, and the lack of dignity of the clergy.

If we put these five criteria together, we can give quite an accurate definition of a "school" dependent on Bérulle. It might be better to avoid using the term "school," which could easily imply almost institutional links between master and disciple, and restrict ourselves to speaking of a spiritual movement in the Catholic Reformation, which is different from that of the Jesuits, Capuchins, Jansenists, etc.

But these criteria are probably not sufficient ....[25]

Because of the transformations made in Bérulle's thinking subsequently, all those we have called "Bérullians" remained faithful to the main orientation, but each one, because of his personality, his work, stressed some particular aspect. Teaching in schools, training priests, evangelizing the poor, going on mission, and praying for the Church are not identical tasks; and it is easy to understand that, depending on the type of work one chooses, one tends to emphasize one or other aspect of the spirituality. And so Bérullism, as its influence spread, ran the risk of splitting up into increasingly autonomous movements, and even of disappearing completely as these merged with other spiritual movements.

A Complex Spirituality

Bérulle, like all founders of spiritual movements, and his disciples, were at the meeting point of multiple influences. We have already stressed this aspect. The synthesis achieved by Bérulle has numerous sources: the pseudo-Denys, the Rheno-Flemish, Canfield, Saint Augustine, the Greek Fathers, Ignatius of Loyola (and Ignatian spirituality revised by the Italian Jesuits), the Spanish Carmelites; but to these we have to add factors which strictly speaking have nothing to do with the history of ideas, but for all that are no less important: the trauma of the Wars of Religion, and the imposed coexistence with what the "pious" [*les dévots*] considered as a heresy (Protestantism), the increase in the power of the monarchy and the questioning of its policies (reasons of State or Catholic policies?), the serious shortcomings of the clergy and the first attempts to remedy them, the existence of a pious [*dévote*] élite, etc.

In this context, a certain number of individuals, who had in common some ill-defined aspirations and were groping around for authentic Christianity, used to meet in parlors or convents. Such meetings gave rise at times to lightly structured "bands"[26] with their own "leaders." This is what happened in the case of Bérulle's spirituality.[27]

While we do not find the expression "French school" too apt, it is nonetheless true that a certain unity can be noted among all the figures we are studying: admiration for Bérulle and Condren, to the point of sometimes quoting them explicitly; meditation on the same texts from Scripture; an apparently pessimistic anthropology but one which in fact puts all its trust in the human person living through Christ; reverence for God, and adherence to the states of Jesus; devotion to Mary; abandonment to the Spirit. All are involved in the Christian education of children, in the interior missions, and in training priests. They are all very attached to the Church, the Mystical Body of Christ, despite the importance they attach to interior piety, to listening to the Spirit, and to the danger of the subjectivism to which it can lead.[28]

THE INFLUENCE OF BÉRULLIANISM (17TH & 18TH CENTURIES): JOHN BAPTIST DE LA SALLE[29]

Among the great founders of the 17th century, John Baptist de La Salle[30] has particular importance by reason of the way in which his Institute – the Society of the Brothers of the Christian Schools

– developed. This educator of poor children, as we shall see, was also very much influenced by the spirituality of Bérulle.

The Life

John Baptist de La Salle was born on 30 April 1651 at Rheims. His father was a magistrate and his mother was from a noble family. At the age of eleven, he received the tonsure; and he was not quite sixteen when he obtained a Canonry at the Rheims Cathedral. He studied theology at Rheims (1669-1670) and then at the seminary of Saint Sulpice, and followed courses at the faculty of theology in Paris for eighteen months. This quite short stay left its mark on him, especially his meeting with Tronson and Leschassier, with whom he maintained relations. It is likely he took interest, among other things, in the catechetical renewal movement and in the appeals to promote the Little Schools. The death of his parents (1671 and 1672) forced him to return to Rheims to administer the family fortune, which he did competently and accurately, before resuming his university studies. He took as his spiritual director Canon Nicolas Roland (1642-1678), still a young priest, but one who already had a reputation for great piety. Made a sub-deacon in 1672 and deacon in 1676, De La Salle was ordained priest at Easter 1678, and obtained his doctorate in theology at the University of Rheims in 1680. This was quite a brilliant beginning to his career, but one that corresponded certainly with a real vocation. As the eldest of the family, John Baptist should not have followed an ecclesiastical career.

In 1678, Roland died, leaving to his spiritual protégé the task of protecting and consolidating the community of the Sisters of the Child Jesus that he had founded in 1675 for poor girls. John Baptist obtained Letters Patent for the Sisters in February 1679, and he administered the material affairs of the house for two years. It was there that he met Adrien Nyel, who had founded schools for poor boys in Rouen and who was trying to do the same thing in Rheims. John Baptist de La Salle made the task easier for him. Two schools were opened shortly thereafter, and John Baptist rented a house near his own for the teachers at Christmastime 1679. In 1680, a third school was opened in this house.

It was in this way that, little by little, the Canon from Rheims discovered the world of schools. He noticed that they functioned badly, through a lack of competent, stable, and pious teachers. What is more, Nyel was often absent. After obtaining advice from the Minim Nicolas Barré, an enthusiastic promoter of popular education, John Baptist invited the teachers to take meals with him. Next he obliged them to spend the whole day in his house. Finally, on 24 June 1681, he decided to lodge them in his own house. From that point on they lived as a community, which was not without its problems. Most of the teachers who were not keen on the direction things were taking, left him. De La Salle's own family did not accept this "promiscuity" with the poor teachers. John Baptist held firm, after a moment of doubt. He was encouraged by the arrival of new teachers and by the success of the schools. On 24 June 1682, he left the family home to live in poor conditions with his disciples in another house. That same year, a school was opened in Rethel, forty kilometers from Rheims, and then others in Guise and Laon.

He made his choice. He would devote himself to schools and give up all his riches. "After much reflection in God's presence, after much prayer and consultation, it seemed evident to him toward the end of the year 1682 ... that God was calling him to take charge of the schools, and since he had to be first at all exercises of the community, he could not assist at the Office (as a Canon) as assiduously as his director demanded."[31]

And so he resigned his Canonry, an appreciable source of revenue. He kept some family money to cover the needs of his brothers, but most of it would be given away to the poor in 1684-1685.

In the course of the winter of 1685-1686, the small community adopted a special form of dress that distinguished them from both seculars and clerics. At the same time, the schoolmasters adopted the title of Brothers of the Christian Schools, substituting the name "teacher" by that of "brother," with a view to community life, but also for an apostolic reason (they were supposed to consider themselves as the elder brothers of their pupils, and be filled with charity for them). They lived together in poverty and shared everything. De La Salle, who was their superior, their confessor, and their spiritual director, sought to train them to a very high level of piety. This is the life he wished to justify in 1690 in his *Memorandum on the Habit*.

The Brothers of Rheims, Guise, Rethel, and Laon held a first assembly in June 1686 at which they pronounced a vow of obedience. The following year, through sentiments of humility and in order to make the congregation more autonomous, De La Salle resigned as superior and had Henry L'Heureux elected in his place. But the Archbishop of Rheims refused this move, and De La Salle was obliged to resume his place at the head of the community. In 1688, he went to Paris at the request of the parish priest of Saint Sulpice, La Barmondière, and took charge of the parish Charity School. But relations were more difficult with the new parish priest Baudrand (appointed in 1689). The overseer of the hosiery workshop next to the school complained that the children working there did not come often enough. De La Salle confronted them and opened a second school in the parish. But then, the Paris schoolmasters began to attack him, complaining of the competition represented by these gratuitous schools. Many Brothers left both in Paris and in Rheims. De La Salle fell seriously ill in 1690; and Brother L'Heureux, who was due to succeed him, died. It was in this difficult context that De La Salle took a vow with two Brothers, Vuyart and Drolin, to remain associated in order to bring about the establishment of the Society of the Christian Schools, by consecrating themselves entirely to the Blessed Trinity (21 November 1691). Shortly before, he had rented a house in the rue de Vaugirard, which became the motherhouse of the Institute.

During a general assembly at Vaugirard (30 May to 6 June 1694), De La Salle and twelve of his companions pronounced perpetual vows of association, stability, and obedience. The Founder once again wanted to resign as superior, but the Brothers elected him superior of the congregation, stipulating that his successor could not be a priest.

At Vaugirard, he pursued his ministry as a priest, celebrating Mass every day in the house chapel, hearing the confessions not only of his Brothers, but also of criminals and profligates who often came from far away to see him. In this way, he acquired a great reputation for resolving difficult cases of conscience. He directed the novitiate while Brother Vuyart taught the young people the art of teaching. But the new parish priest of Saint Sulpice, De La Chétardye, was not happy about this teaching going on outside the jurisdiction of the parish; and De La Salle arranged for the Brothers to move to a former convent, Notre Dame des Dix Vertus (1698).

Here the Institute could grow and increase its influence. De La Salle generally accepted to take charge of schools at the request of bishops, parish priests, hospices, etc. And so he took on schools in Chartres, Calais, Troyes, Avignon, Rouen, Dijon, Marseilles, Grenoble, Versailles, Boulogne-sur-Mer, and Moulins. These were schools for the poor, even if they were mostly accessible to all, something that explains the conflicts with the schoolmasters' corporations. Another concern of his schools – at least of those founded in the South of France (Mende Alès, Les Vans) – is the conversion of Protestants. This work that began in 1707 seems to have proved to be particularly difficult. But De La Salle was involved also with other types of establishments: a boarding school for Irish exiles (Paris, 1699), "seminaries for country schoolmasters" (Rheims, 1687-1690; Paris, 1699; Saint Denis, 1709), Sunday schools in Paris and, at Saint Yon, near Rouen, a fee-charging boarding school, a sort of reformatory school and an "imposed detention section" for "professional profligates."

John Baptist de La Salle also wrote a great deal for the teachers and pupils, as well as books on teaching methodology, prayer books, catechisms, manuals of politeness, and reading texts. His best-known works are *The Rules of Christian Decorum and Civility* (1703) and *The Duties of a Christian to God* (1703).

In 1702, a serious crisis occurred. The parish priest of Saint Sulpice, De La Chétardye, who initially supported the Brothers, began to attack them. He wanted the Brothers to wear ecclesiastical dress and the pupils to act as altar servers at baptisms, weddings, funerals, and Masses, even during school hours. The catechism lessons of the Brothers were competing with those given in the parish. Slanted reports about De La Salle, including a denunciation from De La Chétardye, were sent to the Archbishop of Paris, Cardinal De

Noailles. He was aware of the internal difficulties of the Institute, and the accusations of harshness, stubbornness, and excessive austerity leveled at its superior. He also had some sympathy for the Jansenists, who were opposed by the Brothers of the Christian Schools. For all these reasons, he replaced De La Salle by an ecclesiastical superior of his own choice. The reaction of the Brothers was lively, and the new superior ended up by losing all real authority to the benefit of De La Salle. But there arose other difficulties. The money that should have made possible the purchase of the novitiate house, which had been put on sale, was appropriated by the clergy of Saint Sulpice. The novitiate was then transferred to Faubourg Saint Antoine. The attacks of the Writing Masters that resumed in 1697, became fiercer than ever in 1703, and led to the closure of the school and novitiate in Faubourg Saint Antoine. Faced with this tempest, and to save the school and the training seminary for teachers in the Saint Marcel district, Nicolas Vuyart left the Institute.

The situation became calmer in 1706, and the Brothers returned to the schools of Saint Sulpice. However, the tension between De La Chétardye and De La Salle remained. The parish priest, who was the ecclesiastical director of several women's communities, wanted the right of inspection where the Brothers were concerned. He did not accept either the idea that a layperson could succeed De La Salle as superior of a religious institute. On the other hand, relations were good with Languet de Gergy, an assistant priest of the parish. But there was still more trouble in store. In 1707, the first steps were taken to create a training seminary for schoolmasters at Saint Denis with the help of a number of ecclesiastics trained in the Saint Esprit Seminary founded in 1703 by Poullart des Places. De La Salle was helped by a young cleric, still a minor, called Jean-Charles Clément. But the transaction was contested by the father of Clément and, after a painful process, De La Salle was condemned in 1712 for suborning a minor and extortion of funds. At this point, De La Salle left Paris and, from 1712 to 1714, visited the communities in the South of France. In his absence, an attempt was made to alter the structure of the Institute, making each house practically independent, suppressing the novitiate, and placing the Brothers under the authority of diocesan ecclesiastical superiors. Was De La Chétardye involved in this business? In any case, several Brothers left the Institute.

In Provence, things were no better. Involved in the Jansenist quarrel, De La Salle remained faithful to Roman orthodoxy and lost much support. The novitiate that had just opened in Marseilles closed. Criticism of the austerity of the *Rule* resurfaced. Certain communities (at Mende) even refused to give him lodging. De La Salle felt abandoned by everybody, even by God; and he had doubts about his mission. He sought advice from the Prior of the Grande Chartreuse and from a shepherd woman who lived as a hermit at Parménie, near Grenoble. Both advised him to persevere. The Institute was kept going under the direction of Brother Barthélemy; and, on 1 April 1714, the Brothers of Paris, Versailles, and Saint Denis wrote to him asking him to return as the head of the congregation. De La Salle was surprised. He accepted and returned to Paris in August, and decided to take Brother Barthélemy as his assistant. At the general assembly of 1717, Brother Barthélemy was elected superior. John Baptist de La Salle, having lost almost all his powers, retired gradually, while continuing to take an interest in the Institute. He spent more time in prayer, and died on 7 April 1719, his soul at peace, hoping he had conformed to the will of God in his regard.

Up to this point, the community had lived without approved rules. However, John Baptist de La Salle who lived, for his part, a strict and austere life, was a man of rules. Even if he did not wish to rush things, and preferred to live community life "*ad experimentum*" before laying down laws, he was careful throughout his life to draw up rules for the Institute. At the outset, he had drawn up the *Practice of the Daily Regulation*, which he revised a number of times. We know of the first draft of the *Common Rules*, probably written in 1694, from a manuscript copy of 1705. Another manuscript, dated October 1718, gives a text revised by the Brothers at a General Chapter, and then by De La Salle. The first edition dates from 1726. In line with the trends of the time, the *Rules* go into great detail in all matters, including the timetable, dress, and food. Obedience and regularity are essential virtues; fidelity in the smallest things is required. For De La Salle, regularity maintains peace and union in the Institute, and constitutes the path to perfection and sanctification. But what the *Rules* call interior and exterior "supports" are more important: interior prayer [*oraison*], the presence of God, the spirit of faith, interior recollection, (self) accusation of faults, public drawing attention to others' faults (the advertisement of defects), reddition (an exercise in receiving guidance from the superior), and the way to spend recreation time well. What is essential, however, consists in a number of points on which De La Salle will not give way: the absolute gratuity of schools, the link between the school and catechesis, the lay nature of the congregation, and the autonomy of internal government.

On the death of John Baptist de La Salle, the Brothers of the Christian Schools were present in twenty-two towns in France. They obtained Letters Patent in September 1724, and a Bull of Approbation from Benedict XIII on 7 February 1725. In 1751, there were Lasallian schools in seventy-nine towns, thanks to Brother Timothée, successor of Brother Barthélemy at the head of the Institute. Despite the attempts of certain archbishops (Rouen, Rheims) to have greater control over the congregation by giving it a diocesan status, despite the persistent attacks of the teachers of fee-paying schools (e.g. Abbeville, in 1766), and despite the attacks of enlightened minds against the "*ignorantin*" Brothers, the Institute continued to develop. Under Brother Agathon, in 1779, there were 116 houses, 760 Brothers, and 33,000 pupils. The Institute was most widespread in the Northwest (Normandy, Picardy, North, the Paris basin), and in the Southeast (valley of the Rhône and Languedoc). This represents a spreading out from the first establishments, and a desire to control regions marked by Protestantism. Regarding this latter point, the Brothers sometimes took over schools against the advice of the local population. But on the whole, the remarkable spread of the schools and the absence of any faltering on the eve of the Revolution, prove that the aim pursued by the congregation corresponded to a real need on the part of the common people.

The Spirituality

John Baptist de La Salle is known above all for his pedagogical work. It is not our task to study it here. We shall simply point out its connection with the spirituality of the Founder of the Society of the Christian Schools.

De La Salle is also a great master of the spiritual life. The dedication of a whole life to the promotion of gratuitous schools for the poor was born of fortuitous circumstances: the responsibility as executor of Nicolas Roland's will, the meeting with Adrien Nyel, the realization of the shortcomings of the schoolmasters of the day, the advice of Nicolas Barré, the increasingly close association with the teachers... It was only gradually, but surely in response to some deep desire, that De La Salle came to abandon an ecclesiastical career that had begun so promisingly (canonry, doctorate in theology), in order to choose poverty and the service of poor children. But, despite difficulties and his hesitancy to change the direction of his life in this way, De La Salle saw in these events a call from God.

In fact, he insists frequently on the necessity of docility to the Spirit and even on abandonment to God in order to put oneself more fully under the guidance of the Spirit. "Do you abandon yourselves entirely to this divine Spirit, so that he may ask of God all you need to have for the good of your own soul and for those in your care, and that you act only by him?" is his recommendation to his Brothers.[32] The salvation of each Brother depends on this abandonment to the Spirit who alone will make it possible to think only of the salvation of the children in school. Every word from then on will come only from the Spirit of God, who has taken possession of the Brother and has produced in him the life of grace. Source of a new life, the Spirit is the interior master who makes it possible to know the ways of God and to announce them.

Consequently, one must be attentive to inspirations, to interior impulses, without for all that neglecting the precise rules of discernment of spirits: respect for the diversity of persons and situations, attention to concrete human attachments, conformity to "evangelical values." In this way, fidelity to the Spirit is possible. John Baptist de La Salle in his great devotion to Mary admires in her, above all, constant docility to the Spirit, who led her to admire interiorly all that God had accomplished in her.

It is, in fact, the Spirit of Christ that one has to acquire: "Dispose yourself today, then, to receive Jesus Christ fully, by abandoning yourself entirely to his guidance, and by letting him reign over your whole interior life so absolutely on his part and so dependently on yours, that you may in truth say that it is no longer you who live, but Jesus Christ who lives in you."[33]

We should note the above quotation from *Galatians* 2:20, frequently used by both De La Salle and Bérulle, and which at this precise point, has doubtlessly its source in the first article of *Pietas seminarii* of Olier.

Such a spirituality presupposes a well-rooted Christocentricism. De La Salle speaks often of imitating Christ, of taking him as a model, of following him. But it is not a question of reproducing his behavior only exteriorly. It is frequently a question of conformity to Christ, which supposes true interiorization. For De La Salle, this means participation in the virtues of Christ, that is, by the contemplation of a mystery, adopting the attitude of the Lord for oneself. In fact, the insistence here is on the poverty, humiliation, sufferings, and death of Christ. De La Salle mentions also the persecutions and hostility of the world. One could have the impression that he was engaged in a masochistic search for mortifications, all the more as the first rules in use in the Institute contain very severe practices and excessive austerities – perhaps responsible for the premature death of several Brothers. But with time they were eased. The essential aspect of this is the positive view of these mortifications. De La Salle does not dissociate them from Pauline teaching on the stripping off of the "old man" so that the "new man" can live. He interprets all trials in the light of the Paschal mystery of death and resurrection. This follows closely the line adopted by Bérulle, understood in the same way by Condren, and then by Olier and his successors at Saint Sulpice.

What is involved, therefore, is an interior participation in the mystery of Christ. One can speak in terms of a mystic intention in this wish for life-giving assimilation, for union with Christ. The Holy Spirit, the Spirit of Christ must be at the deepest point in the human person in order to make one live the life of the Son of God:

"The Holy Spirit who dwells in you should penetrate the depths of your souls; it is in them that this Holy Spirit should especially pray. It is in the interior of the soul that this Spirit communicates himself to the soul, and makes known what God asks in order to belong entirely to him."[34]

And the surest way to unite oneself to Christ is sacramental life and especially participation in the Eucharist: "Jesus Christ unites himself to you in Holy Communion to transform you into himself and to make you be one and the same heart and one and the same spirit with him; the interior dispositions that are in him pass over into you and become your own. How happy you should consider yourselves to be in a state where Communion is received very often, where you can always be one, and only one, with Jesus Christ, possess his Spirit, and act only by him."[35]

But this union with Jesus Christ can also be asked for by prayer. The *Method of Interior Prayer* proposed by John Baptist de La Salle is completely in line with this:

"I unite myself to you, divine Jesus, infant God, with an ardent desire to share in the spirit of your holy infancy, in your dispositions, and in the grace which you have merited for me in the mystery of your holy birth. I most humbly beg you, loving child Jesus, to draw me into your divine heart, to impart to me your Holy Spirit, and to endow me with the dispositions you had in the stable at Bethlehem, lying in the crib on hay and straw or in the arms of your holy mother. I earnestly beg you to impart to me the sentiments and affections of humility, docility, submission, and obedience you felt toward your heavenly Father, as well as the feelings of your most holy mother and those of your foster father, the great Saint Joseph. By your grace, Lord, may I have those sentiments and dispositions, toward those who have a right to my obedience. May I be even prepared and disposed to submit with simplicity to all sorts of persons in imitation of you. Grant me, I ask you, Lord, that I share fully in your holy sentiments toward poverty, mortification, and suffering. May I love these and practice them with views of faith, in union with your Spirit and your own dispositions and by the action and the effect of your holy grace, which is at work in me. I promise to cooperate with your grace as far as possible."[36]

United with Christ, the Brother will see everything with the eyes of faith. This involves putting creation in a completely new context: "Not to look upon things but with the eyes of faith is to see created things as God sees them, and as faith requires us to think of them. Thus, when we see a beautiful building, if we wish to consider it only by the eyes of faith, we should remember that all its beauty is external, that its purpose is only to please the senses, and that this beauty is only a passing thing..."[37]

De La Salle, like many masters of spirituality of his time, opposes to such an extent nature and grace, flesh and the spirit, creature and the creator, that it is the world in its entirety and not simply what is "worldly" that is rejected. But the positive side of this is the call to the conversion of the way we see things in order to see the interior aspect of things.

This is what makes it possible for John Baptist de La Salle to recognize Jesus under the poor rags of children, to look at them with God's eyes. That is why it is necessary to devote oneself to their education, to invent, if needs be, new pedagogical means to ensure they are better instructed, never to dissociate academic teaching from Christian instruction. In fact, like Vincent de Paul, De La Salle, at the same time, sees Jesus in the poor and asks us to imitate Jesus by serving them and offering them salvation, which cannot be done without "putting on" Jesus. He explains to his Brothers: "Your words ... because they will be produced by the Spirit of God living in you ... will procure for your disciples the Christian spirit, and in possessing this Spirit, which is the very Spirit of Jesus Christ, they will live that true life which is so valuable to us because it leads surely to eternal life."[38]

And so the Brother must essentially be similar to both the poor and to Christ. This is what explains the Brothers' choice of material poverty and their devotion for the poor Christ, for the very Bérullian mystery of Jesus at his birth and in his childhood: "Be convinced that so long as you remain bound in your heart to poverty and to everything that can humble you, you will do good for souls. The angels of God will make you known and will inspire fathers and mothers to send you their children to be instructed ... But if you do not resemble the newborn Jesus by these two outstanding qualities, you will be little known and little employed, nor will you be loved or appreciated by the poor, and you will never have for them the role of savior, as is proper for you in your work, for you will draw them to God only insofar as you resemble them and Jesus at his birth."[39]

Offering salvation to the poor: the task that falls to schoolmasters is immense, and De La Salle insists often on the zeal necessary to accomplish it. It is in fact a ministry: "Let it be clear, then, in all your conduct toward the children who are entrusted to you that you look upon yourselves as ministers of God, carrying out your ministry with love and a sincere and true zeal, accepting with much patience the difficulties you have to suffer, willing to be despised by others and to be persecuted, even to give your life for Jesus in the fulfillment of your ministry ... You are not only the ministers of God, but also of Jesus Christ and of the Church ... since it is for the Church (which is the body of Jesus Christ) that you work. You have become her ministers according to the order God has given you to dispense his word."[40]

And like Bérulle, like Olier, like so many others, De La Salle asks that the title of Minister of Jesus Christ should not be borne in vain, but that one should be worthy of it through the conformity of one's life with that of Christ.

However, the Brothers are laypersons; and De La Salle was always adamant regarding this, even to the point of refusing to have a cleric as superior of the Institute. This is because, in his view, the mission of educator calls for a person totally dedicated to it (the whole person), and it is not possible for an educator to assume in addition a priestly ministry which De La Salle, with his Saint Sulpice training, did not take lightly. The position adopted by De La Salle is an original one in the Bérullian movement. This movement is sympathetic to the idea of the shared priesthood of the laity, because of the baptismal spirituality that inspires it. But the tendency of the time and the conviction of the necessity of the priestly role and its "eminent dignity" (Olier's expression) led to insistence in particular on this last point, but this fact is far from being a summary of their doctrine as a whole.

On the other hand, the hierarchical view of the world, which grew stronger in the second half of the 17th century with the advent of absolutism, makes it difficult to imagine how any important tasks could be assumed by persons who were not clerics. The complex relations maintained by De La Salle with Saint Sulpice can be explained in the light of this. The founder of the Brothers of the Christian Schools opposed the parish priest Baudrand on the question of clerical dress. He refused to let De La Chétardye have authority over the Brothers. For De La Chétardye, it was unthinkable that a layperson could have charge of souls in a religious community without priests. As we have seen, the conflicts went far. And yet, De La Salle always wanted to have schools in the parish of Saint Sulpice, because he considered Sulpicians to be excellent confessors and spiritual directors. And so, while opposing the hierarchical and clerical tendencies of many Sulpicians, he appreciated the spirituality which inspired them and which drove them to make Jesus live in hearts. All the teaching of Bérulle on the attachment [*l'adhésion*] to Jesus in all his states, as taught at Saint Sulpice, can be found in the writings of De La Salle and applied to lay teachers, with all that this entailed. If this seemed to contradict the view of the Church held by certain Sulpicians, it did not contradict the essential teachings of Bérullianism.

What is at stake is important. The baptismal spirituality proposed by Bérulle had in fact been practiced mostly by priests – but also by the pious members [*les dévots*] of the Company of the Blessed Sacrament who drew their ideas also from other sources, and by the Carmelites who lived in their cloisters away from the world. For De La Salle, this attachment [*l'adhésion*] to the states of Jesus had to be lived out in the humble tasks of a schoolmaster. Neither Vincent de Paul, nor Jean Jacques Olier, nor Charles Démia had envisaged this in such a practical way. Only the Daughters of Charity took up this challenge, but the fact they were women barred them in any case from the priestly ministry. As for the Brothers of the Christian

Schools, they were men, lay, teachers and ministers of Jesus Christ. They show, by seeking to live in conformity with the humble, poor, and suffering Jesus, that Bérullian spirituality can be practiced by lay people in their daily work and that the priestly state is only one way of practicing it, which is not intrinsically superior to the others. Any condition of life, any employment is apostolic, and calls on us to be docile to the Holy Spirit, to the Spirit of Jesus.

That is why all Bérullians, lay or priests, are from a particular point of view close to one another. In particular, they attach great importance to interior prayer [*oraison*]. De La Salle who spent several hours a day in prayer, left behind a lot of teaching on this subject in his *Meditations* (published around 1730) as well as in the *Collection of Various Short Treatises* (1711), revised and developed in the *Explanation of the Method of Interior Prayer* (1739). He insists in particular on the presence of God, interior recollection that is already a form of interior prayer [*oraison*], according to the Carmelite Laurent de la Résurrection, whom De La Salle perhaps met in his convent on the rue de Vaugirard. It means filling oneself with God, uniting oneself interiorly with him, where no words are adequate, through simple attention to the "Other." We should recall that the presence of God had already been proposed by Démia, but perhaps in a less abstract way.

But this teaching is also very practical, as can be seen from the texts of the meditations, which often take realistic considerations as their point of departure. Such as: how to acquit oneself well of one's work as an educator; how to put up with the faults of one's Brothers, etc. It is a view of faith that enables the meditation to rise to a higher level instead of remaining on too prosaic a level. As in Bérulle, high-level considerations must cast light on daily life.

And so, it is the dogma of the Trinity that underlies the prayer on union in the community. Jesus asks for his apostles a union so close "that it resemble the union between the three Divine Persons. It will not be exactly the same, because the three Divine Persons have only one essence, but the union among the apostles would participate in the union of the Trinity in such a way that their union of mind and heart, desired by Jesus Christ for them, would have the same effect as the essential union of the Father, Son, and Holy Spirit. They would all have one and the same convictions, the same will, the same affections, the same maxims and practices... Since God has given you the grace of calling you to live in community, there is nothing that you should more earnestly ask of him than this union of mind and heart with your Brothers."[41]

De La Salle's realism appears also in the different methods he proposes, depending on whether one is meditating on a mystery, a virtue, or a maxim. Depending on the stage one has reached in spiritual life, some will converse by means of multiple reflections and others with few reflections. Others will practice interior prayer [*oraison*] based on simple attention. There is no one way of praying, but the aim is always the same: to make Jesus Christ live in oneself, so as to conform oneself to him and to allow oneself to be guided by his Spirit.

Was De La Salle a Bérullian? A careful study of his sources[42] shows that they are very varied, including even the Jesuits, with whom he had very little contact. "The rules on modesty and good government" find their inspiration in the constitutions of the Company of Jesus. But, most of his inspiration comes from meditation and from practical experience. That is why the Sulpician formation of De La Salle is very important. It is what unites a whole variety of elements in a spirituality that, in this way, may seem Bérullian. But De La Salle also lays great stress on practice. That is why those persons who are in the field, beginning with the Brothers of the Christian Schools themselves, also strongly affect his thinking.

CONCLUSION

We have studied the context in France at the beginning of the 17th century and have outlined the main points of Bérulle's spirituality. That is: Christocentric, but always careful to consider Christ in his relations, his "communications" – as Bérulle prefers to say – to the Father and to the Spirit; attentive to the "states of Jesus," which it is possible for each Christian to live out by allowing oneself to be filled with the Spirit; tending toward contemplation, but at the same time, very apostolic; marked by a desire to restore the priestly state, but in a framework of above all baptismal considerations. Finally, this spirituality appears difficult to define simply. It is always in tension; and it evolved much, seeking first of all to know God through the exercise of the will, a very Ignatian point of view, to end up with a much more contemplative attitude, under the effect of multiple influences, including Saint Teresa and the Spanish Carmelites, as well as the Rheno-Flemish mystics. Only the aim did not change: to show the communications in God and between God and human persons.

And then, we have mentioned a certain number of persons of the 17th century, sometimes of the 18th century, whose spirituality was close to that of Bérulle, and who were indebted mostly to him. These include Carmelites such as Catherine of Jesus, Magdalene of Saint Joseph, Margaret of the Blessed Sacrament; Oratorians such as Bourgoing, Gibieuf, Bertin, Métézeau, Condren, Quarré, Séguenot; founders of other congregations such as Vincent de Paul, Louise de Marillac, Olier, Jean Eudes, Pallu, Démia, John Baptist de La Salle, Grignion de Monfort; others such as Saint Cyran, Boudon, Lambert de La Motte, Laneau, Moye, to name only the most important ones. We have emphasized the apostolic commitment of all these persons. They fought against Protestantism. They attached great importance to works of charity, produced catechisms, ran schools and colleges, were much given to directing consciences, were much involved in missionary work abroad and above all at home, and finally concerned themselves directly with the formation of priests.

After trying to characterize the spirituality of Bérulle, we tried to define a much broader movement that we called Bérullianism. It can be defined as a tone and as common influences (in particular Saint John and Saint Paul, the Greek Fathers, etc.); an anthropology which emphasizes the nothingness [*le néant*] of the human person in order to affirm more strongly the life of Christ in the Christian; a keen awareness of the greatness of God, whom one recognizes by attaching oneself to the states of Jesus; a devotion to Mary, with a solid theological basis; an insistance on the necessity of abandonment to the Spirit; a very strong apostolic commitment; a great sense of the Church and of the priestly role. These are elements common to all we have defined as Bérullians, some elements being stressed more or less in this or that person. We noted also the importance of a "nothingness" trend (*néantisme*), characterized very strongly by the notion of sacrifice, the growing influence of Augustinism, which led many people, in particular the Oratorians, to take the side of those who were beginning to be called "Jansenists"; or the priority given to works of charity following the example of Vincent de Paul. But behind these differences, a certain unity can be clearly seen. It is these common characteristics that go to make up what we commonly call the "French School of Spirituality," and which it seems more just to us to call "Bérullianism."[43]

ANNOTATED BIBLIOGRAPHY

By William Mann, FSC

Benson, Patricia. "The French School: Masculine and Feminine Dimensions " in *Alive for God in Christ Jesus: Proceedings of a Conference on the Contemporary Significance of the French School of Spirituality*, edited by Ronald Bagley et al., 241-255. Buffalo, NY: Saint John Eudes Center, 1995.

Benson provides an idea of the condition of women during this period and a sense of some important relationships between the men who are normally identified as the principal agents of seventeenth-century French spirituality and the women who were their associates.

In citing Natalie Zemon Davis' study of French life [*Society and Culture in Early Modern France* (Stanford, 1975)], she observes that "women suffered for their powerlessness in both Catholic and Protestant lands in the late sixteenth to eighteenth centuries as changes in marriage laws restricted the freedoms of wives even further, as female guilds dwindled, as the female role in middle-level commerce and farm direction contracted, and as the differential between male and female wages increased" (242). However, Benson notes that "women of the privileged class had some influence outside their homes. Some, for instance, founded salons where literary discussions were held, discussions which included women as well as men" (242).

Concerning the "mutual relationships" of the leaders of the French School, it is noted that these "men had relationships with women as did many of the other religious leaders in the seventeenth century." As examples, Benson cites: François de Sales and Jeanne de Chantal; Vincent de Paul and Louise de Marrillac; François de Salignac Fénelon and Madame Guyon; and Pierre de Bérulle, Madame Acarie, and Madeleine de Saint-Joseph (246-249).

Bernier, Paul. "Spirituality of the Counter Reformation" in *Ministry in the Church*, 184-189. Mystic, CT: Twenty-Third Publications, 1992.

"It can be said that the three poles on which Tridentine piety rested were: a revival of sacramental life, the spread and development of Eucharistic devotions and techniques of mental prayer, and an urge to good works and outward activity as a factor in personal sanctification" (185).

"Parish missions were also used to great effect to deepen the religious life of the common people, especially under new congregations like the Oratorians and Vincentians. John Baptist de La Salle set up a number of schools for poor children; and his congregation pioneered a new way of life: dedication without priesthood. The Ursulines and others extended education for girls. Religious education was a priority of many ... The one religious congregation that typified all that was new about the post-Tridentine church, however, was the Company of Jesus" (185-186).

About "the reform of the clergy following the Council of Trent," the author notes that thanks "to the work of men like Cardinal Pierre de Bérulle and Jean-Jacques Olier, a phenomenon known as the French School shaped priestly self-understanding."

These men, and those associated with them, stressed "an exalted notion of the priestly office." In Bérulle's view, "priesthood had two objectives: to worship God and to produce Christ in souls" (186-187).

Some key themes of the French School are identified as: the grandeur of God; the primacy of the Incarnation; the mysteries of Christ's life; sacrificial self-emptying "so that Christ can completely take over"; "forming Christ in the hearts of people" as "the objective of a priest's pastoral care"; and contemplative life at the heart of ministerial activity (187-188).

Brémond, Henri. *A Literary History of Religious Thought in France, Vol. III, The Triumph of Mysticism.* London: Society for Promoting Christian Knowledge, 1936.

This volume in Brémond's monumental *A Literary History of Religious Thought in France* subdivides into three parts. The first concerns Pierre de Bérulle and such related topics as the doctrine of the French School, the origin of the French Oratory of which Bérulle was founder, Bérulle and Vincent de Paul, and the Bérullian Jesuits (1-242). The second concerns the development and evolution of the doctrine, which Brémond considers under such headings as Charles de Condren, toward Bérullism, and the excellence of Jean-Jacques Olier (243-434). And the third concerns the spirit of childhood and devotion to the Child Jesus, Jean Eudes, and devotion to the Sacred Heart (435-572).

It is to Brémond, in this book originally published in 1921, that credit is given for the origin of the term "French School." The volume opens: "The French School – hitherto, whenever this forgotten group of thinkers came to be mentioned, it was termed the Oratorian School, although several of its representatives did not belong to the Oratory ... This school is incontestably the richest, the most original and fertile, of any born in the Golden Age of our religious history, meriting on this score alone the proud name ... assigned to it in these pages – the French School *par excellence*

... truly a School, not of theology, but of the interior life and the highest spirituality" (1).

When considering Bérulle, Brémond notes that "association of piety with dogma seems to have been de Bérulle's especial gift" and that "he followed ... an individual inspiration, for although surrounded by illustrious examples of saintliness, he appears to have been dependent on none, not even on the band of mystics in whose company he soon realized his powers and who helped to bring him into prominence" (9). In commenting on this "band of mystics" – Acarie, Canfield, Coton, Beaucousin, Duval, and Gallemant – Brémond notes, "Bérulle, young and his own master, insensibly became, not the favorite director of the group, but the most active agent to carry out the common decisions, the almoner-in-chief of Mme. Acarie" (10).

In the first part of the book, Brémond explains that Bérulle's spiritual world was Christocentric: "God the Center, to whom all religious life 'should continually move'" (17). "François de Sales had restored devotion, it remained for Bérulle to bring into favor a more essential virtue, the virtue of religion" (26). "Since God is our Father, we must render Him all honor, and that since He is Master, we must fear Him" (29). Wrestling with how to express the meaning of what is to be understood by "virtue of religion," the author juxtaposes the words religion, respect, reverence, admiration, and awe. "The chief fruit of these thoughts is to avow and recognize that the Christians' God is great" (30). Bérulle "assuredly adored the Christ who lived in him, but 'principally' the Christ 'Himself, considered in His Personal Condition'" (42). For Bérulle, "to adhere, whether to God Himself or to the God-Man, is 'to unite ourselves' actively to God or to the God-Man, dwelling and acting in us; to present ourselves, to open our hearts, to surrender ourselves ... to subject ourselves to this Divine presence and action" (108). "The originality of the French School consists in realizing the existence of the Divine Electricity, so to speak, which Providence puts at our disposal, and in desiring and learning how to use it" (118).

In speaking of the Oratory [a brief history of which is provided (133-134)], it is remarked that "the Oratory had for its aim the restoration and glorifying of the state of the priesthood; it must now be added that, to attain this, the Oratorians proposed first of all to show in their lives, and then to spread abroad, the spiritual teaching of M. de Bérulle ... These two elements are in reality one" (146).

Concerning Vincent de Paul, Brémond writes: "He certainly modeled himself, as far as in him lay, on François de Sales ... but, of all his spiritual models, M. de Bérulle appears to have made the profoundest impression on him" (216). "The man of action, the great organizer, confirms by his experience the wholly mystic principles of the master. Even in practical matters, theocentricism is the keynote of his method ... 'for see, my daughters, whoever says charity says God; you are Sisters of Charity, therefore ought you to form yourselves in the image of God'" (217). And finally: "Although deeply marked by Bérullian theocentricism, his fundamental devotion is perhaps to admire the particular workings of Providence, and to abandon himself with closed eyes to the Divine leading" (220).

Brémond quotes Jeanne de Chantal when considering Charles de Condren: "It seems to me that God had given our Blessed Father (François de Sales) to instruct mankind, but that He had rendered this one capable of instructing the angels" (249). And "the most eminent disciple of P. de Condren, his 'double' as we shall see, M. Olier," writes: "His outward being was but a shell of what he appeared to be; his inner man was quite another, living the inward life of Jesus Christ and hidden in him, so that it was rather Jesus Christ living in P. de Condren, than P. de Condren living in himself" (252).

Jean-Jacques Olier's "especial grace and mission was," according to Brémond, "not exactly to popularize Bérullism, but to present it with such limpidity, richness of imagination and fervor that its apparently somewhat difficult metaphysics are placed invitingly in the reach of most readers" (393). And while Jean Eudes "is doubtless more rhythmical and flowing, less abrupt, than the earliest masters of the Oratory, Bérulle, Quarré and Bourgoing, and less impetuous than M. Olier; but on the other hand, one finds less force, less savor, less poetry" (536). Concerning devotion to the Sacred Heart of Jesus of which Eudes is such a great proponent, Brémond observes that this devotion "sprang of necessity from the providential and natural encounter of the two great religious philosophies which, during the first half of the seventeenth century, nourished the inner life of French Catholics – the French School on the one hand, and Devout Humanism on the other" (545).

Buckley, Michael J. "Seventeenth-Century French Spirituality" in *Christian Spirituality: Post-Reformation and Modern*, edited by Louis Dupré and Don E. Salieris (with J. Meyendorff), 28-68. New York: The Crossroad Publishing Company, 1996.

Buckley's essay is essentially "an inquiry into the spirituality of three major figures from the dawn of seventeenth-century France: Francis de Sales, Pierre de Bérulle, and Louis Lallemant" (32). But before addressing what he calls these "three major figures," he notes two other great personages of the opening years of the new century: Benoît de Canfield and Madame Acarie. For Canfield, "Christian perfection is realized as one becomes 'almost wholly absorbed into God and His Absolute Will'" (29). He "simplified the many movements of contemplative development into the progressive identification of the human will with that of God" (29).

But "if Benoît de Canfield nurtured the nascent mysticism of the dawning of the century and Madame Acarie gave it methods of interchange which allowed different traditions to be in communication with one another to mutual enrichment [her salon gatherings], Francis de Sales led the entire century into the world of devotion and the love of God" (32).

Absolutely central to De Sales' theology is "the universal salvific will of God, a will extended to every person" (34). Rather than the prevailing arbitrary theology of predestination, Francis emphasized "the universal salvific will of God" which is "the theological foundation of his piety" (35) and "the archetype which his own compassion would mirror" (36). "The oft-repeated invocation, so characteristic of Salesian piety, bespeaks the central name he gives to God: 'Live, Jesus'" (38).

"The whole of the spirituality of Francis falls within these two movements: the surge that is the human being and the outpouring that is divine providence – the desire and the love of God to transform human beings into his friends, the universal salvific will: 'God willed with a true will that even after Adam's sin, all human beings should be saved, but in a way and by means proper to their natural condition, which is endowed with free will'" (40).

While these references to Canfield, Acarie, and De Sales provide some insight into the spiritual currents in France at the opening of the seventeenth century, Buckley's consideration of Bérulle (42-53) is more relevant for a consideration of the French School of Spirituality. Bérulle was the "founder of the Oratory in France, the great reformer of the secular clergy, the pioneer of the establishment of the Carmelites within France ... the Father of the French School" (42).

In his early writings, he "proposes to guide the soul by way of successive deprivations to the annihilation of the human self and the transforming union with God" (42). Eventually, "the Incarnation would form the optic through which he understood everything" (43). "Incarnation, annihilation, forgetfulness of self, conditions or states, and adherence – the entire subsequent history of Bérulle's contribution to French spirituality could be charted with these topics as coordinates" (43).

The "fundamental movement of the human spirit toward God" for Bérulle is presented as "the recognition in faith of the grandeur that is God and the surrender of oneself to the greatness of God in *l'anéantissement* – a word almost impossible to translate into English, but which catches up the experience of being nothing before the infinite and eternal being of God" (49).

Buckley, in this article, rapidly and succinctly captures key teachings or understandings of Bérulle's spirituality: "the theocentricism which constitutes its major characteristic" (43); a focus on "the Incarnation of the divine Word" (45) and "a spirituality of the Incarnate Word" (46); "the critical experience" of adoration (48) and praise as "the perfect expression of adoration" (49); his consideration of "the spirit, the state, the virtue, the merit of the mystery" of the Incarnate Word which "remain present always" (50); Eucharist in relation to his teachings on Incarnation and Trinity (51); "the muted tones of his Augustinian heritage, the sense of sin and the vastness of the dangers of damnation" (51); "the perfection of adherence" (52); and "the surpassing grandeur of Mary," who "was and remains what every human being is called to: 'a pure capacity for Jesus, filled with Jesus'" (53).

Lastly, Buckley presents as a final significant personage of this period, the Jesuit formator and mystic Louis Lallemant, in whose spiritual teachings centrality is given to the Holy Spirit. "Lallemant is primarily occupied with the Holy Spirit, the indwelling presence and gifts of the Spirit of God and the correlative human responses of contemplation and discernment" (55). As Lallemant wrote, the "two elements of the spiritual life are the purification of the heart and the direction of the Holy Spirit" (57). "Lallemant has but one purpose: to aid the soul to become sensitive to the influence of the Spirit of God. The Spirit above all and within all is to be the guide of the soul" (57-58). And in this teaching Lallemant is focused "on the apostolic life [of the young Jesuits he is forming and educating], the life in union with God given over to ministry in Christ" (60).

Cognet, Louis. "Ecclesiastical Life in France" in *History of the Church 6: The Church in the Age of Absolutism and Enlightenment*, edited by Hubert Jedin and John Dolan and translated by Gunther J. Holst (New York: Crossroad, 1981), 3-106.

Cognet's essay constitutes the first six chapters in a thirty-two chapter study of the post-Reformation Church (1648-1789). "While the Church declined in religious leadership [as a consequence of "the nascent Enlightenment, spreading from Protestant Europe"], it also continued to lose what was left of its prestige in political Europe." (xi, xiii). And the study of spirituality and religiosity during this period, the editors of the book suggest, "shows that there was in the seventeenth and eighteenth century a sort of common search for a Christian answer to the modern world" (xviii-xix).

"Ecclesiastical life in France," a study of Christian renewal from about 1615 to 1715, is the subject masterfully presented by Cognet. "Endeavors by the great Catholic spiritual leaders – Francis de Sales, Benedict of Canfield, Father Coton, Bérulle, and many others – had brought about a Catholic climate whose piety and inward orientation was equal to that of the Reformed Churches. At this time, this *milieu dévot* or *parti dévot*, as it was so called, was still a compact group firmly united by common ideals revolving around the triumph of Catholicism and the defeat of Protestantism" (3-4).

Cognet opens the essay by considering the pitiful state of the secular clergy (bishoprics as "the appendage of the aristocracy" and the priesthood representing the best "possibility for social advancement" for the lower class). "For the purpose of ordination, most bishops were satisfied with mere rudimentary knowledge and only a few demanded even as much as a few days of spiritual retreat" (4-5). "Conditions among members of religious orders were hardly better ... all orders were in need of reform, with the exception of the Carthusians" (6). "Public opinion proved less and less prepared to accept these unbelievable conditions [frequent and blatant scandal]. The court, influenced by the *parti dévot*, began to deal with these matters and civil authorities intervened in order to eliminate the most flagrant abuses" (7).

"The *milieu dévot* which had originated with the Holy League was an extremely eager and active group ... Mme. Acarie and her friends had an efficacious hand in a number of foundations" (10). This group believed "that it was necessary to start all over again by bringing up a new clergy" (20). New seminaries were established by pioneers like Adrien Bourdoise (20); and "the role and influence of the Oratory and the priestly spirituality promoted by Bérulle and his successors, contributed significantly to raising the level of the secular clergy" (21). Jean-Jacques Olier, Vincent de Paul, and Jean Eudes were significant figures in the reform movement concerned with clerical education (22-24).

Cognet then moves on to a masterful coverage of "the origin and development of Jansenism to 1653" and "the Jansenist conflict to 1713" (24-57). He observes about Cornelius Jansen's "remarkable synthesis of the Augustinian concepts of grace and predestination [*Augustinus*]" that "Jansen proceeded from the most extreme positions advocated by Saint Augustine in his first fight against the Pelagians without taking into consideration the long history of their development" (26-27). Consequently, "it was foreseeable that the publication of [the study] would ultimately result in a renewed controversy regarding the question of grace" (31). Cognet not only covers the doctrinal controversy surrounding Jansenism, he considers the topic in light of Church-State, Gallican-Roman, and Jesuit-Oratorian politics.

"Gallicanism and Protestantism" is the subject matter of his next chapter (57-75). "In the beginning of the seventeenth century the theses offered by the majority of French theologians and canonists concerning the function and power of the Pope were clearly aimed at decreasing his importance ... Yet, the French theologians unanimously acknowledged the true primacy of the Pope, his universal authority, and his position as the center of the unity of Christians" (57). "Louis XIV continued his efforts toward religious unity in his realm and to insist upon extending the Concordat of 1516 [an agreement between King Francis I of France and Pope Leo X] to all the areas subject to him, to bishoprics as well as abbeys. This presupposed a broadening of the right of regalia, the spiritual regalia which enabled the King to fill the benefices of a bishop while the bishopric was vacant, and the secular regalia enabling the King to gain possession of the income of vacant bishoprics" (67). "Jansenism unequivocally manifested its opposition to Gallicanism" (67). And concerning Protestantism in France, Cognet states that "intolerance was the rule on both sides ... Protestants and Catholics lived in a sort of mutual fear of each other which frequently led to indelible hatred. It was only within the educated and monied classes that friendly relationships could at times exist" (71).

About the "major trends in seventeenth-century spirituality," Cognet states that "the French *milieu dévot*, which made its appearance after the religious wars and brought about a true renewal of Catholicism, exhibited very clear directions within its spirituality" (75). He goes on to discuss: 1) the growing influence of "the abstract school" (75-77); 2) the "well-balanced concept of Christian mysticism centered around charitable love and a very optimistic view of the possibilities of man" espoused by Francis de Sales (77); 3) "a truly Copernican change in the field of spirituality" advanced by Pierre de Bérulle (and his followers), "recognizing the preeminent significance for the inner life of the secret of Jesus' incarnation and by subsequently concentrating his piety on the person of the Incarnate Word" (77-79); 4) the contribution of the French Jesuits, especially Pierre Coton [the confessor of Henry IV, who "attempts to make piety accessible to the members of the court"] and Louis Lallemant ["a true mystic who ... skillfully combined the most essential themes of Ignatian mysticism with those stemming from Rhenish-Flemish mysticism"] (79); 5) the "practical activities and efficacious undertakings," from deep sentiments of Christian charity, born witness to by people like Vincent de Paul and Louise de Marillac (80-81) and like the members of the *Compagnie du Saint-Sacrement*, whose "virtually omnipresent system of police surveillance" was "used to prevent the laws of the Church from being violated" (81-82); 6) a *milieu catholique* dedicated, above all, to continuing and expanding the educational initiatives begun in the early sixteenth century [the schools of the Jesuits, Oratorians, Port-Royal, Ursuline and Visitation Sisters, and Brothers of the Christian Schools] (83-84); 7) the practice of spiritual reading favoring "works of meditation, moral treatises concerning the duties of daily life, and the hagiographies" (85, 75); and 8) the continued practice of popular Christian life devotions, now especially centered on Mary, the Sacrament of the Altar, Jesus' infancy, and the Sacred Heart (85-86).

Cognet observes that "Catholic renewal, initiated at the beginning of the seventeenth century, was manifested less in the realm of thought than in the area of Christian life and spirituality" (93) and that "one of the reasons for the decline of Scholasticism in the seventeenth century was the success of the Cartesian philosophy" (101). Réné Descartes' *Discourse de la Méthode* (1637) represents in every respect a turning point in Western thought. His search for evidence, aimed for by the application of sharp and clear logic, created a new way of thinking. This gradually crossed over into the religious realm and left behind the cumbersome synthetic dialectics of Scholasticism…" (103).

Cognet, Louis. *Post-Reformation Spirituality*, translated by P. Hepburne Scott. New York: Hawthorne Books, 1959.

"The aim of the present book ... is simply to summarize the history and evolution of the spiritual ideas which led from the Renaissance to what is commonly called the French School" (7). In so doing, Cognet considers post-Reformation spirituality under the following headings: spirituality during the Renaissance and the Reformation (9-25); mysticism in Spain (26-51) and Italy (51-55); the revival of mysticism in France (56-85); the zenith of French spirituality (86-115); and the crisis over mysticism (116-141).

After having observed that the "troubles which so long divided religious France are no doubt enough to explain the fact that spirituality there remained more or less underground [during the 16th century]" and that throughout "this period piety was still trying to find itself and living by importations" (57), Cognet goes on to consider the revival of mysticism in France in the 17th century in terms of the Abstract School and Benet of Canfield

(57-62), Francis de Sales and his first disciples (62-68), Cardinal de Bérulle (69-77), and the Society of Jesus (77-85).

Of Bérulle it is noted that it was, no doubt, partly "under the influence of the picturesque Adrien Bourdoise, parish priest of Saint Nicolas du Chardonnet and founder of one of the first French seminaries" that Bérulle discovers "his vocation of working for the reform of the secular clergy. With that intention, in 1611, he founded the French Oratory" (69).

After what is called "a decisive turning point" sometime "between 1605 and 1608," Bérulle centered his piety entirely on the mystery of the Incarnation. "Jesus was for him not only the way but the goal of the spiritual life" (70).

"On this point [passages in his writings which speak not only of the Incarnation but of God in himself, and especially of the Trinity], his contemplation derives from the Greek Fathers: he likes to see in the life of the Trinity a certain hierarchy in equality, and to insist on the proper role of each person. He sees in the Trinity a sort of pattern which is repeated from end to end of the divine work, as much in Creation as in the Incarnation and the Redemption" (72). In Jesus, "the God-Man, the union of the Godhead and the Manhood presents a sort of fitness, which is as it were the basis of the Incarnation ... With the God-Man a new order, of which Christ is the principle, appears in the world ... The Incarnation, then, modifies in every way the problem of the relations between man and God. Henceforth, it is unthinkable to look for the divinity apart from the Incarnation, that is, from the humanity of Christ" (72).

For Bérulle the Christian's "incorporation into Christ by baptism" is realized by the Christian's interior attitude in what he calls "adherence," which "has its basis in baptismal grace and is therefore part of the very definition of a Christian. But Bérulle is original in requiring the Christian to make a voluntary, conscious effort to conform all his interior life, in every moment of his life, to the interior life of Jesus, to what he calls the states of the Incarnate Word. It is not a matter of mere imitation, which, however perfect it may be, leaves us external to Christ. This conformity must result in a genuine transfusion into us of the very being of Jesus, of his prayer, his feelings, his adoration" (73). This "adherence supposes perfect detachment from all that is not God" (73).

"For while the Christian has to strive with his whole soul to enter into the interior life of Christ [detachment, annihilation, adherence], in the last analysis it is Christ himself who comes to him by grace. Jesus acts in the soul by his spirit, which is the Holy Spirit: adherence is the work of the Spirit in us" (74). "Like most authors of the seventeenth century he insists strongly on inner loyalty to the inspirations of the Holy Spirit" (74).

"The Christian must adhere to the interior states of the Incarnate Word, just as much in simple discursive meditation as in the highest paths of ecstasy. Sometimes Bérulle even seems to confuse contemplation with adherence ... In prayer there is no question of a method, with complicated articulations designed to mask the intellectual poverty of the process; it is a docile abandonment to the illuminations and prayer of the Holy Spirit in us, where prayer and religious inquiry combine in a harmonious synthesis. Such is the principle of Bérulle's 'elevation,' examples of which abound in his works, where lyricism and dialectic depth unite" (75).

In shifting from a presentation of Bérulle to Bérullism, Cognet notes that the prodigious wealth of Bérulle's writing, "by its very luxuriance, embarrassed a public which now [by the mid-1600s] demanded more order and clarity. Bérulle had employed the vocabulary and even the notions of scholasticism, just when scholasticism was being steadily discredited. Bérullism needed to be simplified, pruned down, and presented in the style of the day, and even his most loyal followers realized this and set themselves to do it, convinced that this was the best service they could render to a venerated memory" (87).

Cognet then goes on to consider the work of those "most loyal followers," whom he identifies as: Guillaume Gibieuf (87-89); François Bourgoing (89-90); and Jean Duvergier de Hauranne, abbot of Saint-Cyran (90-93). In addition, those other successors of Bérulle, perceived by the author as a bit "less faithful" in "constructing a synthesis out of Bérullism" by combining them with "views derived from elsewhere," are identified as: Charles de Condren, Bérulle's successor as General of the Oratory (93-95); Jean-Jacques Olier, "the most interesting of all Condren's disciples" (95-97); and Jean Eudes, "those of Bérulle's successors who were able to make a really personal synthesis out of the master's abundance" (97-99).

For Cognet, Vincent de Paul [whose "personal spirituality was in nowise original"], John Baptist de La Salle ["whose thought is very interesting and deserves to be better studied"], and Jacques-Bénigne Bousset ["none of Bérulle's characteristic themes appear in his work"] can hardly be considered Bérullians. (99-100)

A few other personages referenced by Cognet, in his treatment of the influence and the crisis of French mysticism, are: Jean de Bernières, "who sees in Jesus himself the type and model of our abjection" (101); Henri-Marie Boudon, in whose writings "the mysticism of Bernières was combined with the influence of Saint John of the Cross" (102); and Louis Tronson, who was "rightly considered one of the holiest priests of his time" (123-124).

Daniel-Rops, Henri. "An Age of Spiritual Grandeur" in *The Church in the Seventeenth Century*, Vol. 1, translated by J. J. Buckingham. Garden City, NY: Image Books, 1965.

Daniel-Rops attempts, in this volume that is part of his monumental *History of the Catholic Church of Christ*, to give some sense of "the resurgence of the spirit and ideals of Catholicism following the impact of the Protestant Reformation." In the first half of the volume, he focuses attention on "A Builder of the Modern

Church: Saint Vincent de Paul" (13-74) and "An Age of Spiritual Grandeur" (75-175).

An obvious devotee of De Paul, Daniel-Rops refers to him as "the most notable, the most significant man in the whole history of French Catholicism, and perhaps even in the whole Church" (28). "His doctrine was a half-way house between the tenets of his two masters; or, better still, he united them: the ardent mysticism of Bérulle and the devout humanism of Saint Francis de Sales – without forgetting the very precise influences of Saint Ignatius of Loyola. He had more confidence in man than Bérulle had, but even so his method was more rugged than that outlined in [De Sales'] *Introduction to the Devout Life* … For him everything adds up to a fundamental principle, one which governs the metaphysic of the saints, and which Saint Paul stated in unsurpassable words: 'we must live in Christ'" (31).

"His friend and master, Saint Francis de Sales, was the living epitome of the aspirations and tendencies of an age that closed with his own death [1622], the age of Catholic Reformation. Saint Vincent de Paul, on the other hand, laid the foundations of the future – a more lively Christianity, kneaded by the new leaven; a worthy priesthood, conscious of the majesty of its ministry and utterly dedicated; a Church determined to be fraternal, open to all and gentle to the lowly; a human religion in which God speaks to the heart" (73).

For Daniel-Rops, "the first sixty years of the seventeenth century stand out as a period of strength within the Church, an epoch of rare beauty and fruitfulness" (75). And "two main streams of thought are conspicuous: that of Devout Humanism and that of the French School; and to these streams the leaders in the divine quest are all more or less linked. All of them have in common the conviction that, since God is not an idea but three Persons, what is supremely important is to confirm the soul in its relations with those Persons, with whom it must be induced to unite" (80).

The French School had four masters during the period with which Daniel-Rops is concerned: Bérulle, Condren, Olier, and Eudes. "These four men were all related in thought, and they may be spoken of as a school, although there existed perceptible differences between them" (84). Of their disciples or successors, he observes that "many others were recognizable, more or less original in thought, but often blending Bérullism and Salesianism, occasionally perfected by contributions from Italy, Spain and the Netherlands" (86).

This work of Catholic renewal was, for Daniel-Rops, primarily accomplished by: a complete and impressive restoration of the episcopate (90-94); the reform of the regular clergy (95-111); and a prodigious revitalization of communities of religious women and men (112-118). This primarily bore fruit ["the corn springs up"]: in parish missions by which "the mass of Christians might be more thoroughly imbued with the teaching of the Gospel" (118-124), a renewal of faith that was "accompanied quite naturally by countless works of charity" (124-129), and a remarkable expansion in teaching [Jesuits, Somaschi, Theatines, Ursulines, Doctrinaires, Piarists, Sisters of Charity, Sisters of Notre Dame]. (129-134) "It was often extremely difficult to find really competent teachers – a problem which was tackled a little later by Charles Démia, Father Barré, Nicolas Roland, and above all by Saint Jean-Baptiste de La Salle"] (131-132).

There were, in addition, quite remarkable instances of "innumerable pious lay folk of both sexes who were striving toward the same end" (135) in solidarities, congregations, and confraternities "whose activities extended to every sphere" (134-141).

Deville, Raymond. *The French School of Spirituality: An Introduction and Reader*, translated by Agnes Cunningham. Pittsburgh, PA: Duquesne University Press, 1994.

This translation of Deville's important 1987 study of the French School of Spirituality introduces us to Pierre de Bérulle (29-57), Charles de Condren (58-75), Jean-Jacques Olier (76-104), and

Jean Eudes (105-135) as "the most widely recognized masters of the French School," along with John-Baptist de La Salle (171-188), Louis-Marie Grignion de Montfort (189-213), and certain key women of the period (214-235).

When presenting the theology of the French School, Deville asserts that "this teaching, so deeply rooted in the Scriptures and in the Fathers of the Church, was meant as much for laywomen and men and for men and women religious as for priests" (136). He goes on to discuss this theology under five headings: 1) "God is God" [they "reacted to a certain humanism that threatened our awareness of the grandeur, the transcendence, and the holiness of God"] (136-142); 2) "the Spirit of Jesus" ["We are in the hands of the Holy Spirit who rescues us from sin and binds us to Jesus"] (142-143); 3) "the Church: the Body of Christ" ["They understand that the liturgical year enables us to re-live the states and the mysteries of Jesus. The preaching and commitment of missionaries, under the inspiration of the apostolic Spirit of Jesus, are the continuation and the fulfillment of the mission of the Incarnate Word"] (143-144); 4) "the priests of Jesus" ["Olier stated as an objective for those 'who come to be formed' in his ideal seminary: to come 'to know who they are in the Church of God and to understand the grace of their state'"] (144-147); and 5) "Mary, Mother of Jesus" ["In Olier's eyes, Mary was the model of the clergy. The Feast of the Presentation of the Virgin, on 21 November, was essential in the seminary's liturgy. It was the occasion on which the priests and seminarians renewed their commitments to God and to the Church"] (147-149). And he concludes this presentation by noting that "Bérulle and his followers brought a strong sense of pedagogy to the transmission of their spiritual doctrine" and, in their efforts "to have Jesus formed" in their disciples, "promoted this formation through certain practical means and did not hesitate to create new pedagogical methods" (149). "All the devotions of the French School, in the last analysis, are only means to reach its one, single goal: to help women and men who seek to respond to the Lord's call in their lives" (151).

In referring to John-Baptist de La Salle as one of the "heirs to the Bérulle School" (171), Deville asserts that De La Salle's "genius consisted in understanding and repeating ceaselessly to his Brothers that their 'labor' was bound to their 'state,' and was totally apostolic. Thus, they were to live under the influence and 'the action' of the Holy Spirit. This Spirit was, as Bérulle and his followers had asserted, nothing other than the Spirit of Jesus, a Spirit both filial and apostolic" (178). The "mystical christocentrism of the Bérulle School" ["Jesus Living in Us!"], asserts Deville, found expression in De La Salle's teachings on prayer (178).

Finally, the chapter on the role of women in the French School (214-235) did not exist in the 1987 French edition of the book. "On close examination," Deville writes, "relatively few women can be attached to the Bérulle School in the strict sense. Madeleine de Saint-Joseph would surely be the best example of one of them. We might also include Madame Acarie, although she, rather, shaped Bérulle to a certain degree, before becoming more or less his disciple ... However, a good number of women, both lay and religious, were truly sources of inspiration for the followers of Bérulle" (216-217).

"It was through Madeleine de Saint-Joseph [the first French prioress of the first monastery of Discalced Carmelite nuns in France] that Bérulle's doctrines of adoration, of mystical christocentricism through 'adherence' to the states and mysteries of Jesus, and of particular devotion to the Mother of God were spread through Carmelite monasteries in France" (221). Louise de Marillac [co-foundress with Vincent de Paul of the Society of the Daughters of Charity] "was at home with words and ideas that belong strictly to the Bérulle School: 'honor' God and 'Jesus in his mysteries,' the 'holy Humanity of Jesus' and other similar expressions. She had a great devotion to the feast of the Annunciation, the Incarnation of the Word; to the infancy of Christ, to the Eucharist, and to the grace of Baptism. Like Condren and Olier, she considered the feast of Pentecost as one of the greatest of all feasts" (224). Deville asserts that Louise "was marked by the tradition of the Bérulle School, even though she was influenced by many other spiritual movements as well" (224).

Deville, Raymond. "The French School of Spirituality" in *Jesus Living in Mary: Handbook of the Spirituality of Saint Louis Marie de Montfort*, edited by Patrick Gaffney, 437-457. Bay Shore, NY: Montfort Publications, 1995.

This article is divided into five parts. Under the heading of introduction (437-439), Deville notes that Louis Marie de Montfort "is one of the best heirs and witnesses of the French School" and that "although Montfort retained the main characteristics of the doctrine and teaching methods of Cardinal de Bérulle and Jean-Jacques Olier – among the many and varied spiritual writers used as his sources – he did it in a way distinctively his own" (437). The movement "had many followers: Saint Louis de Montfort, Saint John Baptist de La Salle, Louis Lallemant, etc." (438). The "characteristics of the movement" are identified as: a deep mystical experience, a stress on specific aspects of Christian faith and living, a mystical sense of the Church as the Body of Christ, a certain Augustinian view of the human person, an extremely strong apostolic and missionary commitment, a detailed and well-adapted method of instructing others, and special concern for the dignity of priests (438).

Under the heading of background (439-440), Deville observes that "France was going through a period of revival after the wars of religion ... It was in this period that the bourgeoisie grew. Its members lived rather close to the aristocracy, and the Christian renewal started with them. Most of those called 'devout people' belonged to the 'middle class'" (439). "The missionary renewal went hand in hand with an educational renewal and with a multitude of apostolic initiatives" [Madame Acarie's drawing room, the Company of the Blessed Sacrament, the Tuesday Conferences of Vincent de Paul] (439-440).

Under the heading of leaders of the movement (440-446), Deville identifies: Bérulle and Condren as its founders (440-441); Jean

Eudes as a great missionary in the tradition of the Oratory (441-442); and Olier as, in the words of Henri Brémond, "an excellent follower and witness of Bérulle's teaching" (442-444). He then goes on to consider some Jesuit spiritual writers ["There was a mystical trend among the French Jesuits between 1610 and 1650, a current that had some kinship with the Bérullian movement"] (444-445) and the role of women in the French school ["Prominent members among the French school were influenced by women ... The most authentic Bérullian may have been Mother Madeleine de Saint Joseph"] (445-446).

Under the heading of spiritual doctrine, spirit, and pedagogy (446-455), Deville develops the point under six headings: 1) Christ-centeredness, the spirit of religion, adoration ["Our Lord Jesus Christ came into the world to bring reverence and love for his Father and to establish his kingdom and his religion" (446)]; 2) mystical Christ-centeredness, Christian living, the Spirit of Jesus ["All the members of the school (Olier, J. Eudes, J. B. de La Salle, Louis de Montfort) experienced the influence of the Holy Spirit, called the 'Spirit of Jesus,' and spoke a great deal about Him" (447)]; 3) the sense of the Church ["We will draw attention to the fact that their broad and deeply mystical vision of the Church contrasts starkly with the idea, then prevalent, of a Church with a highly centralized government preoccupied with legalistic matters" (449)]; 4) the French school and missionary activity [the controversies between Catholics and Protestants; "home missions"; the renewal of liturgy, teaching of catechism, and promotion of charitable activities in the parishes; care of the poor and reform of prostitutes; the training of priests; the education of youth; and the foreign missions (450-451)]; 5) a specific pedagogy [prayer, examinations of conscience, spiritual reading (453)]; and 6) the pessimism of the French school [They "took an excessively pessimistic view of human nature ... insisting of the sinful condition of man and his nothingness as a created being" (454)].

Finally, Deville, under the heading of Louis Marie de Montfort as the last of the great Bérullians (455-457), cites as examples: 1)

Montfort "developed in his own highly distinctive way Bérulle's idea of Christ-centeredness"; 2) "When he considers at length the mysteries of Jesus lived in Mary and communicated by her, he develops Olier's thought and prayer"; 3) "Like many of his contemporaries, Montfort was a missionary, but his activity was as firmly based on theology as [was that of] Jean Eudes"; and 4) "Like Bérulle and Olier before him, Montfort maintains that the severe austerity of the Cross and of death to self is tempered by the love and maternal presence of Mary" (456-457).

Deville, Raymond. "The Seventeenth-Century School of French Spirituality" in *Vincentian Heritage*, Vol. 11, No. 1 (1990), 17-28.

This article by the then Superior General of the Sulpicians [which also appears as "Alive for God in Christ Jesus" in *Alive for God in Christ Jesus: Proceedings of a Conference on the Contemporary Significance of the French School of Spirituality* (Buffalo, 1995)] is divided into three parts: 1) an introduction "to some of the main representatives of the French school"; 2) an introduction "to the principal characteristics of the movement"; and 3) an introduction to "some texts typical of the school" (18).

During [the seventeenth century in France] "the entire French church experienced a genuine, strong regeneration that was spiritual, apostolic and missionary – altogether" (17-18). The "leaders of the French renewal" who are identified as the principal figures of the French School are Pierre de Bérulle, Charles de Condren, Jean-Jacques Olier, and Jean Eudes (18). A "contemporary, a good friend of the foregoing, and recognized as a spiritual leader in France – perhaps the premier leader – Vincent de Paul does not belong to the Bérullians in the strict sense. On the other hand, it seems possible to speak of ... Louis-Marie Grignion de Montfort ... and John Baptist de La Salle ... as belonging to that branch because both were trained by the Sulpicians (Olier's disciples) and their teaching is very Bérullian" (18).

"Although Bérulle is the father of the Bérullian school, it is absolutely necessary to say a few words about Francis de Sales ... His influence was extraordinary. He may be regarded by all our communities as a common father, a proto-father, from whom each of us has descended – Visitandines, Vincentians, Daughters of Charity, Sulpicians, Brothers of the Christian Schools" (18).

Of Bérulle it could be said "that he progressed through an evolution which consisted of three distinct stages": 1) the period of his devotion to reading and accumulating knowledge; 2) the period when "under the influence of Madame Acarie and her circle" he "came in contact with the Rheno-Flemish movement of returning to God alone in adoration of His fullness – God is God, the rest is nothing – theocentricism"; and 3) the period "centered on the person of Jesus, the Incarnate Word … a mystical Christocentricism leading to identification with Jesus: 'It is no longer I who live but Jesus who lives in me (Gal 2:20)'" (20).

"The entire movement of spiritual and apostolic renewal [being studied in this article] had the following characteristics": 1) "a profound spiritual experience" ["frequent reading of and meditation on the Scriptures"]; 2) "an emphasis on certain aspects of the Christian faith and life" [the grandeur of God, communion in the states and mysteries of Jesus, devotion to the Spirit]; 3) "a mystical sense of the Church, the Body of Christ, the continuation and fulfillment of the life of Jesus"; 4) "a very theological and sound … devotion to our Lady … the mother of the Incarnate Word"; 5) an anthropology that was "Augustinian and pessimistic on the one hand, yet very positive and optimistic on the other"; 6) "a vigorous, apostolic missionary commitment" [pastoral reform, renewal of religious life, parish life, catechetics, and works of charity]; and 7) a "concern for the dignity of priests, their sanctity, and their formation" ["the urgency of a profound coherence between his life and his ministry"] (22-23).

Diefendorf, Barbara B. *From Penitence to Charity: Pious Women and the Catholic Reformation in Paris*. New York: Oxford University Press, 2004.

Diefendorf presents the reader with two interesting and complementary readings or interpretations of the Catholic Reformation in Paris at end of the 16th century and during the first half of the 17th century: 1) she makes more visible the significant role played by pious women in the spiritual life of a nation and 2) she presents a socio-religious axis of interpretation (nuanced and scholarly) for the evolution from a spirituality grounded in acts of penitence to one grounded in acts of charity.

The Catholic Reformation is presented as "a complex movement that changed and evolved over time," one that required "a vast grassroots effort ... to fund and administer new religious institutions, to catechize an ignorant populace, fortify believers, and revivify the faith" (251). Pious women, especially in Paris, played an essential role in doing this. "Circumstances in Paris were more favorable to female achievement than they were elsewhere in Europe. Two women, Marie de Medici and Anne of Austria, served as queen regent during the first half of the seventeenth century, and aristocratic women had a prominent place in their courts. Proximity to literary salons where women played an important part made it easier for Parisian women to take on other leadership roles, as did the mores of elite society, which allowed women a relatively large role in family strategies and domestic affairs" (17, 250, 251).

The active role of women, to return to Diefendorf's first "reading or interpretation," has often been eclipsed (8, 245-246); and credit has more often been given to "a handful of great men" [Vincent de Paul (203, 243), Francis de Sales (176-183), Pierre de Bérulle (279)]. "The Catholic revival was the product of a vast collaboration between clerics and lay people, women and men" (246).

The active mysticism (82) and the deep spirituality of the salon gatherings in the home of Barbe Acarie (78-80, 85-86) is highlighted. "As one historian has noted, we should not see the hôtel Acarie as a sort of devout salon, however distinguished the company: 'It was in effect much less a place for meetings and conversations than a center of spiritual action'" (80). Too often Acarie, herself, "is depicted as animating the devout circle that gathered at her Paris townhouse through her mystical visions rather than her forceful personality, hard work, and organizational skills" (246). "In the case of Barbe Acarie, the charitable and managerial activities in which she took part ... clearly were accompanied by a deepening and interiorizing of her spirituality" (41). "Within months of his first meetings with Acarie, Dom Beaucousin had confided to André Duval that he found in his penitent 'a hidden treasure,' adding that 'however well versed he was in spiritual things, he was learning more from her, than she was from him'" (83).

The second of Diefendorf's "readings or interpretations" concerns a shift in spirituality related to two significant historical events: the League (the Holy Union in 1576-1594 of Catholic nobles fearful, among other things, of a Huguenot king) and the Fronde (the struggle in 1648-1653 between the king and the princes, nobility, and law courts). "If the spirituality of the Catholic revival evolved in response to an internal dynamic, it also evolved in response to the external forces of economic depression and war" (243).

This is the backdrop provided (League and Fronde) for the "evolution from one dominant spirituality to the other," a turning – rooted in an "impulse to charity" – from "penitential asceticism" (enclosure, hair shirts, flagellation, and other forms of corporal discipline) in emulation of the self-sacrificial love of Christ toward more "internalized forms of deliberate self-humiliation and denial of will" (19).

"We might theorize ... that it was the trauma of the League more than the admonitions pronounced by its preachers that opened the path to the internalized spirituality of reformed Catholicism. When the League began, both supporters of the Holy Union and opponents who remained faithful to the Crown agreed that the disasters from which France was suffering were products of human sinfulness and signs of God's wrath" (48). "The wars of the Holy League ignited the ideal of a Catholic crusade.

A crusading mentality found expression in communal rites of penitence and an ecstatic and apocalyptic spirituality" (7). "Heroic asceticism ... was one spiritual path that was not barred from women ... their deeds, and the publicity given these deeds, had important consequences for the spiritual and material propagation of the Catholic Reformation in France" (8). "Far from satisfying the desire for reclusive new convents [over 60% of the 48 new religious houses founded in Paris for women between 1604 and 1650 were traditional, contemplative convents] into which to retreat into penitential austerity from a dangerous and sinful world, the example of the Carmelites and Capucines appears to have stimulated additional foundations. The rapid growth of the Carmelite order was itself a response to this new demand for the contemplative life" (135, 140).

By the time that mid-century was approaching, great social, economic, and political stresses were once again on the rise in the nation; and these same stresses, over a period of years, caused a new generation of "pious women to readjust their religious values, and a preference for charitable service came to supplant penitential asceticism as the dominant spiritual mode" (8). "Like their mothers, the younger women remained profoundly Christocentric in their piety, and yet they tended to attach themselves more to the example of the living Christ as teacher and friend to the poor than to the agonies of his passion that had been the favorite subjects of meditation for Barbe Acarie and her peers" (241). "The Fronde was not a religious war and so, for all the damage it caused, did not prompt apocalyptic visions and acts of penitential atonement" (244). "New spiritual currents, including the more optimistic love of God preached by François de Sales, also diminished the prestige of religious austerity" (171, 13); and "Vincent de Paul and other popular preachers made charity to one's neighbor the frequent theme of their eloquent sermons" (14). "Where the generation of women who helped initiate the Catholic revival hoped to save the lost souls of the heretic Protestants by their prayers, their daughters sought to shoulder a still broader mission in becoming apostles to the poor" (13). "By the mid-seventeenth century, the Parisian dévote was no longer a solitary figure, moving silently among religious services, meditative devotions, and her personal and private charities. Rather, she was enmeshed in collaborative efforts on a new scale" (235).

Fleming, David A. "French School of Spirituality" in *The Fire and the Cloud: An Anthology of Catholic Spirituality*, 268-275. New York: Paulist Press, 1978.

The personages identified in this essay as belonging to the French School are: Pierre de Bérulle, Charles de Condren, Jean-Jacques Olier, Vincent de Paul, Jean Eudes, and Louis Grignion de Montfort (268-269).

While acknowledging "significant differences among the authors of the French School," the following are identified as common themes: "a radical Christocentricism, an emphasis on the 'virtue of religion' leading to an attitude of honor and respect rather than intimacy in prayer, an insistence on identification of the individual Christian with the interior 'states' [attitudes, feelings, outlooks] of Christ, and a strong devotion to Mary and the Eucharist. The French School was permeated with a pessimistic Augustinian view of man and sin, which gave rise to a great stress on abnegation and 'annihilation'" (269).

"In order to familiarize readers with [the works of these authors] ... a collection of relatively brief quotations" from the works of one or other of the various authors is provided (269).

Gautier, Jean. "Oratorian Spirituality" in *Some Schools of Catholic Spirituality*, edited by Jean Gautier and translated by Kathryn Sullivan, 290-346. New York: Desclee Company, 1959.

Gauthier asserts that Pierrre de Bérulle, Charles de Condren, Jean-Jacques Olier, and Jean Eudes – the four "great" founders of the French School of Spirituality – were men of many contrasts. "It takes time to discover beyond their grand composure, their infinite tenderness of heart" (290).

About Bérulle who introduced the Oratory into France, he says that "everything helped to prepare him for God's service. He placed himself under the direction of the Jesuits; he followed courses at the Sorbonne. Between times he converted heretics, exposed alleged saints, went often to the hotel Acarie where he met very famous mystics..." (292). Condren, who was to succeed Bérulle as superior of the Oratory, "absorbed [Bérulle's] teaching, making it his own in his own way" (294). Olier is principally known as one of the great founders of French seminaries; but he also merits being remembered for his great work as the pastor of the Parish of Saint Sulpice. "At that time the parish covered a lot of territory ... He visited every home. He reorganized the catechism classes for children and adults ... He gave new impetus to workers' associations. He founded thirty-four parish schools and several libraries for the circulation of spiritual books. He introduced preparatory retreats for engaged couples ... He enhanced the splendor of church ceremonies, worked against the custom of dueling, procured tools for poor workers, arranged for aid to be given discretely to those who were ashamed of their poverty, restored several convents..." (295-296). Eudes "preached many missions, converted his province [Normandy], took charge of repentant young girls ... and, at the same time, he introduced the faithful to devotion to the Sacred Heart" (297).

When Pius IX canonized Jean Eudes in 1925, the Pope "paid homage not only to the saint himself but also to the School of Spirituality to which he belonged and many of whose great intellects he influenced such as Bossuet, Bourgoing ..., Vincent de Paul ..., Grignion of Montfort..., John Baptist de La Salle..." (298).

The spiritual doctrine of the French School is guided by "the principle that we are created by God and made in His image so to Him we must return (this is Augustinian Exemplarism); that, here below, we ought to begin to be what we will be eternally in heaven: a host in adoration of the three divine Persons..." (298). Gauthier develops this doctrine by considering the teachings of the French School in terms of: the Trinity (299-302), adoration

(302-306), Christ as the perfect adorer (306-308), adherence to the Incarnate Word (308-312), and abnegation or disappropriation (312-315). He then goes on to examine the "means of adherence" and identifies the "principal ones" as: prayer (315-320), Mass and Communion (320-323), and the fulfillment of the duties of one's state in union with Jesus (323-331).

Gauthier also discusses the special devotions of the French School: the Child Jesus, the Interior of Jesus, the Sacred Heart, Our Lady, and the angels and saints (331-338); and he concludes by answering the question "What, then is man?" with "the definition given by Bérulle: 'Man is an angel. He is an animal. He is a miracle. He is a center. He is a world. He is a god. He is nothing surrounded by God. He is in need of God. He is capable of God and filled with God, if he wishes'" (346).

Glendon, Lowell M. "French School of Spirituality" in *The New Dictionary of Catholic Spirituality*, edited by Michael Downey, 420-423. Collegeville, MN: The Liturgical Press, 1993.

The principal figures of the Bérullian or French School are identified as Bérulle, Condren, Olier, and Eudes. Others identified as significant are Madeleine of Saint-Joseph, John Baptist de La Salle, and Grignion de Montfort (420).

The author, whose 1983 doctoral dissertation at Fordham University studied Olier's "theological and spiritual anthropology," identifies the important movements of the period within which the French School emerged as renewal in biblical and patristic studies, the Catholic-Counter Reformation [in particular, the reform of the clergy], and a strong reaction to "devout humanism" (420).

The chief characteristics of the writings of French-School authors are identified as: "a strong contemplative, apostolic, and missionary spirit"; "a Trinitarian theology"; and a deep belief that we "are called to commune intimately with the divine life of the Father, Son, and Holy Spirit" (420).

A number of major themes that emerged among its principal figures are: theocentricism ["God in Jesus" as "the center of our spiritual universe"]; Christocentricism ["a strong reading of Gal 2:20"]; Mary [the temple, the altar, the icon of Jesus]; and priesthood ["the renewal of the faithful would bear fruit only if their pastors were deeply spiritual and learned men"]. Although their view of the church and ordained priesthood was hierarchical, "they had a clear sense of both the priesthood of the faithful and the universal call to holiness" (420-421).

Some of their still-valid insights are identified by Glendon as a "heightened sense of the transcendence of God" and "the essential connection between the life of prayer and ministry" (422). He concludes by stating that "the French School offers a powerful spiritual synthesis, blending profound mysticism with zeal and energy for reform" (422).

Healey, Charles J. "French Spirituality in the Seventeenth Century" in *Christian Spirituality: An Introduction to the Heritage*, 277-312. Staten Island, NY: Society of Saint Paul, 2009.

Healey, like most others, considers the seventeenth century to be "the golden age of spirituality in France" (278). He presents Madame Barbe Acarie, and the influential group that gathered around her, as central "in the early stages of the revival of mysticism in France" – Benet of Canfield, Dom Beaucousin, André Duval, Pierre Coton, Jacques Gallemant, Jean de Bretigny, Pierre de Bérulle, Michel de Marillac, and the Marquise de Maignelay (279).

Francis de Sales in his *Introduction to the Devout Life* "sought to extend the pursuit of perfection far beyond a monastic context. Through his hands the piety of the cloister was brought into the world and monastic devotion was transformed into popular devotion" (284-285).

About Bérulle and the French School, Healey believes that "the Bérulle School would be a more apt term, since French spirituality in this period is broader than the French School" (287). After noting that Bérulle's "special vocation was to work for the education and sanctification of the diocesan clergy" (288), Healey goes on to present some characteristics of his thought: God's transcendence and grandeur, "adherence" to Christ, the "states" of the Incarnate Word ["they are past in execution, but they are present in their virtue"], abnegation or annihilation, and Mary's role as Mother of the Incarnate Word (289-290).

The other great masters of the French School are identified as Charles de Condren, Jean-Jacques Olier [who "places a particular emphasis on Christ's Eucharistic state"], and Jean Eudes (291-296). Vincent de Paul, who practiced a piety that "was simple, non-mystical, Christocentric and oriented to action," was influenced by Francis de Sales as well as Bérulle (296-297). And two later religious leaders "who had close ties with the French School were ... John Baptist de La Salle ... and Louis Marie Grignion de Montfort" (298). The section on the French School concludes by mentioning "the important role women [Madame Acarie, Mother Agnes of Jesus, Marie Rousseau, Marie des Vallées, Louise de Marillac, Madeleine de Saint-Joseph] played in the development of its spiritual tradition" (298).

This chapter of the book concludes with some consideration of Jansenism and Quietism (299-305), French Jesuit School (305-308), French Missionaries (309-311), Maurists (310), and Armand Jean de Rancé (311).

Minton, Ann. "The Spirituality of Bérulle: A New Look" in *Spirituality Today*, Vol. 36, No. 3 (Fall 1984), 210-219.

The author, whose 1979 doctoral dissertation at New York University is entitled *The Figure of Christ in the Writings of Pierre de Bérulle (1575-1629)*, describes the writings of Bérulle as verbose, repetitive, inaccessible, ponderous, and jarring (210). They reflect a "negative description of the human condition" (210), but he did share "some of the hope in human achievement brought to the fore by the Renaissance" (211). Minton proposes, with many cautions, that his writings are worthy of a new reading. His interests are not so different from our own. He was concerned with reform of the church, the relationship between church and state, and personal holiness (211).

Concerning the reform of the church, he started out to bring others [Calvinists] back to the church (212); but he ended up trying to make Catholics different. For him the church was "a gathering of contemplatives," a vision "more appropriate for the cloister than the world" (217). While remaining very active throughout his life, he gradually attempted in the latter portion of his life to detach himself "from the ultimate success or failure of his works." "What was essential was the grace of God" (216).

Concerning the relationship of state and church, he saw "the ruler as special representative of Christ the King on earth" and "the state at the service of the church." Neither conception is "readily useful to us." However, he "always considered it necessary to judge the political order by the gospel" (218).

Concerning personal holiness, Bérulle "considered the goal of life to be conformity of his actions with God's will. Hence, he needed to find the will of God" (211). Self-love and self-delusion were understood as the obstacles to this, and he emphasized "denial of self in order to be united with God" (212). Hence, the need to be one with Christ, "completely dependent on grace," "entering into Christ and the mysteries of his life" (214).

His own plans for personal holiness did not unfold as he wished. "Much of his emphasis upon emptiness, silence, and adoration bespeak a loss of confidence in himself and a lack of clarity about what he was supposed to do." This has often been misinterpreted throughout the course of the past few centuries. It really was "a way of being silent and poor before God when we are unaware of, and unable to control, what we will become" (218). His life's journey led him gradually to understand that instead of doing good for God he needed to allow God to do good in him (213).

His life was based "upon his radical dependence upon God, and he allowed himself to be led in prayer to become the man God envisioned" (219). He strove to be faithful to "Jesus the priest, whose mission was to bring all people back to the Father" (217). Access to God was, for him, through Jesus, "the path to God, the one who reveals the Father." "Jesus is," for him, "the true center of the world [à la Copernicus] and the world ought to be in continual movement toward him" (213).

Pourrat, Pierre. *Christian Spirituality, Vol. 3: Later Developments, From the Renaissance to Jansenism*, translated by W. H. Mitchell. London: Burns, Oates, and Washbourne, 1927.

From the middle of the 15th until the middle of the 17th centuries, the "principle of nationality asserted itself in a very remarkable way"; and consequently "the schools of spirituality of [what is here called] the later period no longer appear simply as belonging to religious families, as in the Middle Ages, but as those of nations [Spain, Italy, France]" (v).

The book opens with the Renaissance and the systematization of the spiritual life [the development of methodological prayer] (1-22); examines Ignatian spirituality (23-48), Christian and devout humanism (49-62), Protestant mysticism (63-79), the Spanish Schools (80-229), the Italian School (230-271), Francis de Sales who was able to unite the devout life with "the business of the world" (272-321); and, more importantly for our purposes, concludes with a presentation of the French School of Spirituality (322-401).

The principal agent or protagonist of the French School is presented as Bérulle; and his most famous disciples being Olier, Condren, Vincent de Paul, Eudes, and Grignion de Montfort (328). A movement, by inclination, directed more toward "Saint Paul and Saint Augustine than to" Francis de Sales (323). "Nothing could turn away [Bérulle's] mind from meditation on the 'mystery of Christ'; neither the affairs of court in which he mingled nor honors" (334).

The general characteristics of the spirituality of the French School are identified as "devotion to the Word Incarnate, a special regard for the virtue of religion, and the Augustinian conception of grace" (335).

"Jesus, says Bérulle, is the true sun, toward which the earth and our hearts ought to be continually moving" (335). Jesus is proposed by Bérulle to be "the living ideal of sanctity" (336). Devotion to Jesus, it was perceived, had "grown cold." The "Doctors of the Sorbonne in the 15th and 16th centuries had put a veil – a philosophical veil – over the divine face of Jesus, and had thus concealed him from the eyes of many" (337).

The virtue of religion "remembers, above all, that the adoration of God is the Christian's first and principal duty" (338). For Bérulle, it consists above all in adoration; there "is nothing in him [Jesus] which does not deserve homage, honor, deep reverence and submission from all creatures in heaven, on earth, and in hell (Phil 2:10). It is the most essential act and exercise of religion, the first obligation of the creature toward God, the chief duty of the Christian toward Jesus Christ our Savior" (340).

Augustinianism is the third characteristic of the French School (341). Augustine's "teaching as to grace captivated" Bérulle. The blessing of grace "is actual, because Christians live from his [the Incarnate Word's] divinely human and humanly divine life, which is communicated to them through the Holy Spirit, thus making each of them another Jesus Christ" (342). "Grace, the divine life within us, thereby exercises its sovereignty over us. Bérulle, whilst of course maintaining human freedom, places the efficacy of grace in high relief. In the accomplishment of good works he sees primarily the action of God." To understand this, "we must know that there are two kinds of operations employed in the sanctification of the soul: the work of God in the soul and that of the soul toward God. The first is what we call grace, and the second virtue" (342-343).

The Bérullian doctrines of abnegation and of adherence to Christ are grounded in the understanding that the "more we renounce ourselves, the more we cling to Christ, and vice versa. Union with Christ and renunciation of self take place in us at the same time. Logical priority, however, belongs to renunciation" (346). "In order to have no other being or life but in Jesus, we must annihilate all that is of ourselves and of Adam within us" (347). Furthermore, this "total mortification, without which Jesus cannot live completely in us, is much more the effect of the Holy Spirit than it is the result of our efforts" (356). "Our cleaving unto Christ will be the best means of mortifying our evil instincts ... We cling to Jesus, we unite ourselves to him by participation in his mysteries" (356-357). "The mysteries of Jesus Christ are in some circumstances past, and in another way they remain and are present and perpetual. They are past as regards their performance but they are present as regards their virtue, and their virtue never passes, nor will the love with which they have been accomplished ever pass. The spirit, then, the state, the virtue, the merit of the mystery is always present" (357-358). Real Christians need "to reproduce within themselves the mysteries of Christ" (359).

The Blessed Virgin, priesthood, and public devotion to the Sacred Heart also merit mention. First, as everything in the Christian religion, according to the French School, needs to be looked upon from the point of view of Jesus, "it especially inspires devotion to the Blessed Virgin and the saints" (369). According to Bérulle, the "best way of making manifest our devotion to the Blessed Virgin is to contemplate the life of Jesus in her and to strive to participate in it" (369). Second, the chief end of the French School "was the sanctification of the clergy ... It looked at the priesthood in its relationship to the mystery of the Incarnation" (382). "There is between Jesus and his priest a kind of identification. Jesus preaches by the mouth of the priest, consecrates this great work of the holy Eucharist through his ministry, remits sins through him. The acts of the priest are the very acts of Christ" (383). Third, "the Feast of the Heart of Jesus ... of Saint Jean Eudes ... appears to be a transformation of the Bérullian Feast of Jesus and the Sulpician Feast of the Interior of Jesus" (395).

"Saint Jean Eudes loved to think of the Heart of Jesus as the symbol of the interior of the divine Master, as portraying all the collective dispositions of his soul" (398). "The Bérullian School, when it speaks of the interior of Jesus, does not forget to remind us that it is the Holy Spirit who is its author and principle. It is he who created in the soul of Christ those most perfect dispositions which we so admire" (401).

Rodrigue, Jean-Guy. "Religious Life in France during the Sixteenth and Seventeenth Centuries" in *Spirituality in the Time of John Baptist de La Salle*, edited by Robert Berger, 3-79. Landover, MD: Lasallian Publications, 1999.

In the first part of the essay (4-8), Rodrigue provides a description of the state of the church in France at the end of the sixteenth century: forty years of civil war; "the system of *commendam*"; the decadence of religion ["church wealth was equal to more than one third of the total wealth of the entire nation"]; "a worldly clergy ... incapable of performing worthy priestly functions"; "priests, especially in the rural areas ... given over to wine, lust, and witchcraft"; and a "separation of external appearances from personal morality." "A true and profound interior spirit was not generally considered fundamental to the Christian life. The task, therefore, of spiritual leaders and their followers was to bring to life this essential element of Christianity" (6).

However, "there were [also] some points of light that were shining and giving promise for a bright future" as the seventeenth century opened into what has become known as "the golden age of spirituality" in France (6). A few austere religious orders (Capuchins and Carthusians) were inspiring people by their heroic lives, their mysticism, and their mortification, silence, and solitude (6). The Jesuits, who arrived in France in 1552, "developed an ever-growing influence among the aristocracy and the bourgeoisie" (7). The importance of the salon of Madame Acarie, the founding of the French Carmel (1604), the arrival of the Ursulines (1596), the founding of the Daughters of Notre Dame (1607) and the Sisters of Notre Dame de Lorraine (1618), and the availability of "pious writing of every kind" [translations of books by German, Flemish, Spanish, and Italian writers] is noted (7-8).

The second part of the essay (8-52) concerns the influence and the writings of the spiritual leaders of France in the early seventeenth century and, more specifically of the French School. Among those discussed by Rodrigue are: Madame Acarie (1566-1618) and the Abstract School ["The single goal of this Abstract School of spirituality was to achieve perfect conformity of the human will with the will of God"] (8-10); Francis de Sales (1567-1622) and the Salesian synthesis [De Sales recognized "that the day-to-day living of ... faith not only enriched" one's own life "but also benefited society at large"] (10-20); Pierre de Bérulle (1575-1629) and the Bérullian synthesis ["He put Jesus 'as the true center of the world' in place of the human person, whom the devout humanists had placed as the center of Christian life, and he proclaimed that 'the world should be in continuous movement toward him"] (21-33); and the spiritual leaders who developed Bérullian spirituality (33-52). Principal among this latter group are: Charles de Condren (1588-1641) and the spirituality of annihilation ["All contact with God begins with the annihilation of the creature"]; Jean-Jacques Olier (1608-1657) and the Sulpicians ["It is sometimes difficult to determine exactly which thoughts are his and which are those of his followers"]; and Jean Eudes (1601-1680) and devotion to the Hearts of Jesus and Mary ["The heart of Jesus living in Mary and the heart of Mary living in Jesus achieve the highest level of the mystery of Christ that is completely accomplished in her. He lives in her and she in him; she exists only as one with him"].

Rodrigue underscores, in the third part of the essay (52-60), De La Salle's contact at an early age with "several devout priests": Canon Pierre Dozer, Vicar General, Chancellor of the University of Rheims, and a relative of the De La Salle family; his year and a half at the seminary of Saint Sulpice "under the spiritual direction of Louis Tronson and François Leschassier"; and his close relationship with Canon Nicolas Roland (52-53). De La Salle, the priest, commits himself to "the spiritual and moral formation of children" through the means of the school and gave himself wholeheartedly to "the spiritual formation of the teachers" [He prepared the Brothers "for their encounter with the students by making them aware of the presence and action of God in their own lives, and of the dignity and importance of the mission that God had entrusted to them"] (54).

Rodrigue asserts that "De La Salle did not develop any major themes that were not already present in the writings of the French School of spirituality and of other spiritual leaders of his time. His genius was to adapt these themes in order to create a spirituality for Christian teachers" (54). The themes used to demonstrate "how De La Salle was influenced by the French School" were his understandings: 1) of God [God is infinitely superior to all created things and there is nothing "more natural than for a creature to offer God the homage of adoration and of abandonment to the divine will" (55)]; 2) of Christ ["the mystery of the Incarnation at the center of the Christian life" (56)]; 3) of the action of the Holy Spirit ["I desire that the Spirit of Jesus Christ be the Spirit of my spirit and the life of my life" (57)]; and 4) of the human person before God [While "De La Salle does not accept this dark view of the creature before God, he does insist on the need to recognize 'the dependence we have on God and how underserving we are of enjoying the benefits and happiness of his holy presence'" (58)].

The fourth part of the essay (60-79) presents De La Salle's spirituality, unquestionably influenced by the major themes of the French School and, yet, "uniquely suited for persons who are dedicated to the Christian education of children, especially the working class and the poor" (60). Rodrigue presents De La Salle as a man "focused on doing the will of God"; a man searching "for this will in the events of his life as they occurred"; "a man of God, imbued with faith and zeal for God's glory," who encouraged his disciples to teach by "example more than by words" (61).

The key themes of this Lasallian spirituality for teachers is summarized as: 1) called by God to do God's work as co-workers with God (62-64); 2) especially for the poor and in service of the church, building up the body of Christ (64-66); 3) by the action of the Holy Spirit, in the spirit of faith and zeal (66-70); 4) living the interior life, based on asceticism, attention to the presence of God, and total abandonment to the guidance of the Spirit (70-75); and 5) lived out in association, obedient and faithful observance of the *Rule*, and a keen awareness of the union between "the duties of your profession and those that refer to your salvation and perfection" (75-79).

Sheldrake, Philip. "Seventeenth-Century French Spirituality" in *A Brief History of Spirituality*, 133-138. Malden, MA: Blackwell Publishing, 2007.

This section of Sheldrake's telling of "the story of Christian spirituality from its origins in the New Testament to the present day" is a brief but excellent overview of the period. "Seventeenth-century France saw a second outstanding wave of Catholic reform, influenced in part by elements of Ignatian spirituality [123-128] and Carmelite mysticism [128-131] but with flavors of its own. However, the notion of a single 'French School' of spirituality is misleading. There were several distinct and even conflicting trends. The two most theoretically developed traditions were associated with Pierre de Bérulle (1575-1629), and with Francis de Sales (1567-1622) and Jeanne de Chantal (1572-1641). There was another strand associated with Vincent de Paul and Louise de Marillac, and two movements that were criticized as heretical, Jansensim and Quietism" (133-134).

Bérulle's was "a Christ-centered, incarnational spirituality," and "he taught that the Christian was drawn into the glory of God-as-Trinity through Christ. By God-in-Christ's 'humiliation' in, first becoming human and, second, in suffering death, humanity was granted access to God's life" (134). Jean-Jacques Olier, Bérulle's disciple, "gave attention to personal experience of Jesus Christ and to the role of the Holy Spirit in uniting us to Christ" (135). He identifies as the "other important figures in the same broad school": Jean Eudes, Louis Grignion de Montfort, and John Baptist de La Salle (135).

Sheldrake asserts that Francis de Sales "had a more significant impact than Bérulle." With Jeanne de Chantal, they "developed a form of spirituality suitable for men and women in every context, not least the everyday world" (135). Their spirituality "emphasized God in creation and God's love for all humanity and desire to forgive anyone who sought reconciliation" (136).

The heart of the spiritual tradition of Vincent de Paul and Louise de Marillac lay in "union with God through serving Christ in the poor" (136). Jansenists "taught predestination and a limited atonement" (137). Quietism, and particularly "the circle of Madame Guyon," associated itself with "the notion of an excessively passive understanding of contemplation and with a total surrender to the initiative of God" (137).

Tavard, George H. "The Christology of the Mystics," *Theological Studies* 42 (1981): 561-579.

Tavard believes that "the witness of the mystics" through the ages [e.g., Pierre de Bérulle] is "a valid and valuable source" for the study of Christology. He observes that the "presence of Christ has been seen, in recent Christologies, as a presence in society, a societal presence, rather than as a presence within the self, a spiritual presence apprehended in the inner life" (561); and to correct what he perceives as an imbalance, the author here examines "the centrality of Christ in mystical experience" in medieval and post-Reformation Catholic mysticism (561).

"Medieval piety is Christocentric" (561); and the "first half of the Middle Ages pays more attention to the divinity of the Lord ... the Christ of glory" (562). "The summit of contemplation is identified with the experience of Mount Tabor, where the humanity of Jesus is perceived as transfigured by the radiance of his divinity" (563). Some authors even insist "on the transitory aspect of the humanity of Jesus [its function is temporary]" (563). The

Franciscans and Dominicans of the thirteenth century, however, "spread a Christocentric piety centered on the humanity of Jesus" (565). Tavard notes a "tension, latent in late-medieval devotion, between the divine and the human aspects of Jesus" (567). And with the *devotio moderna*, one "seeks, above all, friendship with Jesus: 'When Jesus is present, all goes well and nothing seems difficult; but when Jesus is absent, everything is hard'" (568).

In the period of the Counter Reformation, "continuity is patent in the centrality given to the image of Christ [Ignatius of Loyola, Teresa of Avila, John of the Cross]"; and, yet, a new Christological style emerges (570). "Influenced by the Fathers of the Church, by the medieval scholastics, especially Thomas Aquinas and Bonaventure, by the Christian Neoplatonism of Denys and, more recently, of Giovanni Pico della Mirandola (1463-1494), by the Rhineland Mystics, and by the mystical tradition of the Reformed Carmel, the major authors of the French School build a powerful synthesis of theology and piety in their spiritual writings. The founder of the movement, Cardinal Pierre de Bérulle (1575-1629), teaches a highly original Christocentric spirituality. I would venture to call it the first modern Christology" (571).

"Bérulle effectively achieved a synthesis of experience and theological reflection ... the profundity of his thought derived from sharp insights joined to prolonged reflection ... his chief interest was in the participation of man in the inner attitudes of Jesus as Word Incarnate" (572). "The heart of the Bérullian conception of spiritual life rests in a meditation on the 'states of Jesus,' which brings about a participation in them. Bérulle does not believe that the 'states' in which the humanity of Jesus lived have now passed away forever. Since they are the states of the God-Man, they have persisted ... they will perdure forever" (575). Contemplation "of the states of Jesus belongs to the very heart of Christian life. The faithful are called to participate in the mysteries of the Incarnation, not as these were visible in the earthly life of Jesus but as they are eternalized in his ever-present states" (575).

Tavard concludes this essay on the contribution of "the witness of the mystics" to Christology by stating: "It is in his divinity as the eternal Word, manifested to the human heart by the power of the Holy Spirit, that Jesus speaks inwardly. Neglect of this would immeasurably impoverish the Church's Christology" (579).

Terrien, Lawrence. "The French School and the Reform of the Clergy" in *Alive for God in Christ Jesus: Proceedings of a Conference on the Contemporary Significance of the French School of Spirituality*, edited by Ronald Bagley et al., 225-236. Buffalo, NY: Saint John Eudes Center, 1995.

Terrien provides a good sense of the fragility of priests and, in so doing, clarifies why "one of the most significant contributions of the French School to the Church was its concerted effort to reform the clergy." Citing passages from Vincent de Paul about priests being "the Church's worst enemies" and Jean-Jacques Olier about there being "so few genuine priests and pastors in the Church that the hearts of the faithful remain burdened with ignorance and sin" (225), the author goes on to explain that "one of the most obvious difficulties of the period was the process of the selection of bishops and their consistent absence from their own dioceses. Often nominated by the king for political reasons, many had little religious motivation and even less interest in staying at home to visit parishes and supervise their clergy" (226).

First of all, there were too many priests ["the ratio may have been as high as one priest for ten or twelve lay people" in Paris and "an overall ratio of one priest to 200 or 400 people" throughout France]. "Many of the clergy were desperately poor ... they turned to simony ... complaints about drunkenness were frequent ... another complaint ... was the frequency of concubinage ... another frequently cited problem was ignorance ... the intellectual training was very haphazard" (227-228). The Council of Trent attempted "to transform the life of the clergy ... legislation required bishops to stay at home in their dioceses and ... to make visitations of the parishes." Dioceses had to open seminaries to provide intellectual training and "a serious spiritual formation for diocesan candidates" (230).

The members of the French School, in implementing the vision of the Council of Trent, brought their "own points of emphasis" to the training of the clergy: 1) the "notion of hierarchical mediation is very strong" [a "very exalted language about the offices of bishop and priest" ... separating "the priest dramatically from his people" and placing "him in a role of mediator between God and humanity"] (232-233); 2) "a call to conversion and spiritual renewal for those who hold offices in the church," a positive consequence of this exalted view of the clergy (233); 3) "a strong sense of the centrality of the Word of God in the spiritual life of all Christians and especially of the ordained" ["Olier includes the injunction that the residents of the seminary ought always to carry the book of the gospels on their person"] (233); 4) a "close association of the ordained ministry with the person of Christ" (234); 5) a "strong emphasis on the apostolic spirit and a sense of mission" [re-Christianizing France] (234); and 6) "a strong sense of the priesthood of all the faithful" ["The faithful on earth who are in Jesus Christ, sharing in all his titles and all his honors, are," wrote Olier, "made priests like him in the depths of their souls"] (234-235).

Terrien goes on, then, to specify some of the specific efforts of the members of the French School to help with the reform of the clergy: Pierre de Bérulle, who in 1611 introduced the Oratory into France to assist in the formation of the clergy; Vincent de Paul, who in 1631 began to preach retreats to men preparing for ordination, in 1633 began his "Tuesday conferences" for the clergy, and in 1635 and 1643 established seminaries; Jean Eudes, who in 1643 established a seminary in Normandy; and Jean-Jacques Olier, who in 1642 established the Seminary of Saint Sulpice in Paris and in 1651 "proposed to the Assembly of the clergy in France a set of guidelines for how to establish a seminary in a diocese" (235-236).

Thayer, David D. "The French School" in *The Bloomsbury Guide to Christian Spirituality*, edited by Richard Woods and Peter Tyler, 171-183. London: Bloomsbury Publishing, 2012.

Thayer, who is the Sulpician editor-in-chief of the *Bulletin de Saint-Sulpice*, asserts that when "one explores all of the writings of the four primary figures of the founding of the French School [Pierre de Bérulle, Charles de Condren, Jean-Jacques Olier, and Jean Eudes] ... certain words begin to sing a certain melody: mysteries and states, *anéantissement* ["an absolute dependency upon God, the self-destruction of sin and the re-clothing of the Christian in Christ in redemption"], apostolic spirit. They provide a *leitmotif* of concerns and themes that can be clustered within the framework of Father Olier's method of prayer [adoration, communion, and co-operation]" (172).

Adoration (Jesus before my eyes): "The goal of the spiritual life ... is to be lost in God, to live in a manner that God is all in all" (173). "Given the reality of sin, however, such communion with God is not possible except through a second divine action [the Incarnation]" (173). "Entrance into the life of Jesus, living the spirit of Jesus, then is the focal activity of prayer, life and ministry from the perspective of the French School" (174).

Communion (Jesus in my heart): The Christian life is "a continuation and fulfillment of the life of Jesus" (175). "Through the graces given in baptism, the Christian ["the French School insists upon protecting the liberty of each Christian"] begins to live the life chosen for him or her for the sake of the Church" (173).

Co-operation (Jesus in my hands): "Enlivened by the Holy Spirit, all Christians are called to live as Jesus does, participate in His life for the glory of God alone" (177). In conjunction with this point, Thayer goes on to identify the main "devotions and spiritual disciplines" which, for the French School, helped one "learn to co-operate more fully with the actions of the Holy Spirit" (177). These are identified as: 1) devotion to the Eucharist [through this sacrament "each one of us enters more deeply into union with God" (177)]; 2) the Cross ["devotion to the Cross entailed not the choosing of crosses for oneself, but embracing the crosses that arose from one's state in life" (178)]; 3) devotion to the Word of God ["their writings are inspired and infused with the Scriptures, especially the texts of Saint John and Saint Paul" (178)]; 4) devotion to Mary ["all devotion to Mary deepens devotion to Christ enabling us to live His spirit more fully" (179)]; 5) spiritual direction ["a ministry of discerning the presence of the Spirit of Jesus alive in those who came to them for direction" (180)]; and 6) ésprit apostolique ["influenced by the same Spirit that settled upon the Apostles, called forth in the same way to proclaim the good news of salvation to the ends of the earth" (180-181)].

In addition, a number of others are identified by Thayer as members of the French School: Gaston de Renty, John Baptist de La Salle, and Louis-Marie Grignion de Montfort (171). On the other hand, Vincent de Paul "differs enough from that of the major figures of the French School to suggest that he is a cousin rather than a direct member" (171, 182).

The "primary members of the French School of Spirituality," he contends, "sought to reform the church in France in light of the Council of Trent not by being a pillar of fire that led it forward, but by concentrating on the hearth of its daily life [breathing "the dark coals of a church dissipated by … a mediocre fervor … into fiery renewal"]" (172).

"It [the French School] teaches its own forms of meditative prayer, as witnessed in the writings of Jean Eudes, John Baptist de La Salle, and Jean-Jacques Olier, to name a few. Its pedagogy is institutionalized, especially in its seminaries ["the priest was called to be an icon through which others might learn the path of holiness"] and its schools" (181).

Thompson, Edward Healy. *The Life of Jean-Jacques Olier: Founder of the Seminary of Saint Sulpice*. London: Burns and Oates, 1886.

This biography of Jean-Jacques Olier does not really analyze or synthesize the teachings of the French School or Olier's role within the development of what has come to be known as its spirituality. However, it does provide a good sense of the pastoral reforms initiated by Olier as pastor of the parish of Saint Sulpice and of the seminary for the training of the clergy he founded within the parish; and it was in this seminary that John Baptist spent the formative years of 1670-1672 and to this parish that De La Salle and his Brother teachers moved in 1688 as their school-work expanded outside the diocese of Rheims.

Only three topics from the biography are here presented: Olier as pastor, Olier as founder, and Olier with his associates. Firstly, Olier found the parish of Saint Sulpice in a "frightful state" when he arrived as pastor. "In the first half of the 17th century the immorality and impiety which prevailed in Europe … had reached its height in Paris … Of this demoralization and corruption the quarter of Paris in which M. Olier was called to minister was a flagrant exemplification": hatred of priests and a contempt for religious; monstrous impiety, superstition, and sorcery; violence, debauchery, and general lawlessness; eating and drinking to excess (181-184). The clergy of the parish did not devote sufficient time to their duties, and Olier "was to find no support or consolation in the great laymen of his parish" (184-185). "And this, then, was the soil which the servant of God was called to cultivate, and these were his fellow-laborers and patrons!" (186).

He "collected the ladies of the parish together for the purpose of consulting them on the pious and charitable works which should be established" (190). "Looking upon his parish as God's estate which he was set to administer, M. Olier divided it into eight districts" (192). He began "instituting a series of catechetical instructions in twelve different localities besides the parish church" (201). "Besides making provision for the poor and ignorant, his care was also directed to those who occupied the position of teachers, many of whom were themselves in need of instruction" (204). Before long, "this parish, lately so forsaken of God … had become the scene of what had all the appearance of a perpetual mission, and the result was a wonderful revival of piety and fervor among the people" (212).

Secondly, "the Church in the 17th century was richly adorned with men distinguished for erudition and culture; what she needed was a race of ecclesiastics animated with the true spirit of their order [the ecclesiastical state], who by their fervor and zeal should awaken the slumbering fires of piety among the more learned members of the body" (418). It was the intention of its founder that the seminary of Saint Sulpice be "a model and precedent for all other similar institutions in France and elsewhere" (418). "The first stone of the seminary was solemnly laid by M. Olier himself, in the name of her whom he loved to style Queen of the Clergy" (432). Of her, Olier wrote, that "it pleased God that, although His holy Mother was not present at the Last Supper, inasmuch as she was not to receive the visible priesthood … nevertheless she should be present in the *caenaculum* on Whitsunday, there to receive the Apostolic grace and spirit; that is to say, the spirit of zeal for the glory of God and the salvation of men." And it was to keep this great and beautiful truth ever before the minds, as it were, before the very eyes of the students, that [Olier] placed in the seminary "chapel a large painting by Le Brun, representing the Queen of the Clergy receiving the plentitude of the Holy Spirit on the day of Pentecost, which from her is distributed among the Apostles and the assembled faithful" (436).

Thirdly, two observations will be made about a consecration by Olier with his first associates. The first observation concerns the "irrevocable engagement made" in 1642 by Olier and his associates. No sooner had they "entered their retreat than they proceeded to consecrate themselves to His service and form themselves into a community. As the end which they proposed to themselves was to promote the glory of the Most Holy Trinity by means of the sacerdotal order" … they bound "themselves by a sacred promise never to abandon or to depart from the design which it has pleased God to manifest to them and even to confirm by numerous signs" (131-132, 239).

The second of these two observations is about the annual renewal of one's consecration to be made by the clergy of Saint Sulpice on the principal feast of the seminary, the Presentation of the Blessed Virgin, "when every ecclesiastic in the house was to make a solemn renewal of his engagements, uniting himself in spirit to the interior dispositions of the daughter of the King of kings when she left her people and her father's house" (440-441). "The first occasion of this observance was on November 21, 1650, about which time ... the new chapel [of the seminary] was consecrated" (441).

Thompson, William M. "A Study of Bérulle's Christic Spirituality" in *Jesus, Lord and Savior: A Theopathic Christology and Soteriology*, by William M. Thompson, 226-249. Mahwah, NJ: Paulist Press, 1980.

In this book, Thompson is attempting "to raise to the level of conscious awareness the approaches one can take" to the study of Christology "and thus foster some measure of awareness of and responsibility for their limits and adequacies" (3). This chapter of the book (226-249), which also appears in *The American Benedictine Review 28* (1978), is his "attempt to introduce and renew interest in the remarkable Christocentric spirituality of Pierre de Bérulle and the seventeenth-century French school of spirituality" for, according to Thompson, Bérulle "is one of the few figures in Christian history to explore systematically the Christ-experience, quite consciously attempting a living synthesis between Christology and spirituality" (11).

"What gives Bérulle a particular contemporaneity," writes Thompson, "is the fact that he stands at that turning point in Western history when our 'isolated self' ... begins to emerge. Man, in the seventeenth century, owing to the new awareness of reason as a self-liberating instrument and its fruitful application to technology, was beginning to understand the good life as an individualistic project of self-realization" (226). "Bérulle's own 'Copernican Revolution' – as he called it – was a quite conscious attempt to present a Christian alternative to this closure of the self. In essence, through the exemplarist categories of Neo-Platonism, Bérulle denies that man is a being locked up in himself because God is not a self-enclosed, isolated Being. In Bérulle we find a systematic exploration of the Relational God of Christianity and the Christian notion of the person as a living relation to this God" (227).

"Bérulle writes on two fronts ... On the one hand, he writes to the Renaissance humanists, the precursors of our more over-differentiated isolated ego ... and ... Bérulle's second front is that of the 'spiritualists,' who under the influence of an excessive Neo-Platonism, would bypass the humanity of Jesus in the spiritual life" (227). Bérulle asserts: "Jesus is the true Center of the world, and the world must be in continual movement toward him" (227).

"Thus, while in the realm of dogmatics the situation [of his time] was not a particularly favorable one for developments in Christology, Bérulle may be taken as the foremost representative of a more creative undercurrent, in whom the critique of Scholasticism, the recovery of the biblical-patristic tradition, and the 'mystical invasion' converged. All three factors would enable him to produce an impressive Christological synthesis" (230).

"I am convinced," writes Thompson, "that [Bérulle's] own theological spirituality represents a creative attempt, not to reject, but to critique and integrate into a higher synthesis the concerns of this new consciousness..." (233). "What Bérulle was searching for was a more wholistic view of human consciousness, one not viewing man in an isolated state, but seeking to find him in his totality; not as cut off from his ground and source of meaning, but in his fundamental relationship to God. This seems Bérulle's fundamental intuition, and the key to his thought."

Thompson, William M., editor. *Bérulle and the French School*, translated by Lowell Glendon. Mawah, NJ: Paulist Press, 1989.

The book provides us with: 1) an introduction to the French School, principally its historical aspects, theology, and spirituality; 2) principal texts from the writings of Bérulle, Olier, Eudes, and

Madeleine de Saint-Joseph; and 3) a retrospective evaluation of its relationship to our own times. The editor grounds the exposition in the "belief that human experience opens out, in and through God, to a Mystery inviting adoration. This intersection between human experience and Divine Mystery is something of a master key in the French School, unlocking the meaning of humanity and indicating why our French mystics had such a concentrated fascination for the mystery of the Incarnation (for our mystics, the most intensive and unsurpassable expression of that intersection)" (xii).

Some factors presented as the historical context of the French School were the political maneuverings of the times, the challenges of the Protestant reformation, the influence of the Renaissance, a new pluralism, breakthroughs in mystical and spiritual thought and practice, advances in patristic and biblical studies, an increasingly appreciated literature of mysticism and spirituality, enormous pastoral renewal, and priestly reform (3-13).

The French School is presented as profoundly Christocentric, usually "viewing the Incarnation as a prolongation of the Trinitarian mystery on earth" (35). Madeline's "special charism was to emphasize the role of the humanity of Jesus as the never-to-be-bypassed mediator of union with God" (37). The pathway to heaven is, in shorthand, one marked by adoration, abasement, adherence to Jesus, annihilation, abnegation, and acceptance and fulfillment of apostolic duty (xvi).

Some characteristics or accents of the French School are presented as: its Trinitarian theocentricism, a refusal to separate theology from spirituality, viewing the Christian life "as one of struggle between attunement to our deepest being and the opposing failure to remain so attuned" (39), the renewal of the priesthood, the restoration of the spirit of religion, the importance of Mary, devotion to the saints, empathic Augustinianism, an accent both on anéantissement [the 'no-saying' to any attitude or action away from Christ], and on ecclesial and pastoral practice.

Bérulle is presented as "a reformer, seeking to renew the church especially through a spiritual transformation" (56). He "held a high view of the lay state. For him, as for the entire French School of this period, all were called to perfection, each through his or her own unique manner of participating in the various states of Christ" (58). Olier "nicely conjoins the spirituality of the priest with that of the Christian and mystical life in general" (63). After identifying John Baptist de La Salle among the later members of the French School who were "clearly Bérullian," the author notes that while its male representatives "had stressed the priesthood as the experienced example of commitment to Jesus" De La Salle "stressed the apostolate of teaching as an expression of Jesus" (81).

Their greatest contribution is presented as having "wed a deep spirituality to ecclesiology and ministry" (87). "The rooting of all genuine renewal in the contemplative transformation of the heart seems as fresh today as it must have seemed back then" (88).

Thompson, William M. "The Christocentric Trinitarianism of the French School of Spirituality" in *Alive for God in Christ Jesus: Proceedings of a Conference on the Contemporary Significance of the French School of Spirituality*, edited by Ronald Bagley et al., 29-44. Buffalo, NY: Saint John Eudes Center, 1995.

Thompson opens his essay with the observation that Christocentric Trinitarianism is the very center, or heart, of the French School and refers to its four principals [Pierre de Bérulle, Madeleine of Saint Joseph, Jean Jacques Olier, and Jean Eudes] as the "supergalaxy" of the School. Others identified as "associates of this galaxy" are: Charles de Condren, Gaston de Renty, John Baptist de La Salle, Louis Grignion de Montfort, and the Ursuline Marie of the Incarnation]. "At its source our School represents a decisive return to the style of life and thought characteristic of those four (Holy Writ, creed, liturgy, and Fathers). The Gospel of John and the Pauline Letters, each emphatically Christocentric and Trinitarian, literally permeate the French School" (29).

The author goes on to identify a few typical features of the Trinitarian Christocentricism of the School: 1) the "development of the tradition of meditating on the mysteries and states of Jesus" [our participation in Christ Jesus] (35); 2) a faithful representation of "the biblical view that Jesus' life and work is an epiphany, a divine-human reality" ["Jesus' humanity and divinity are distinct but never separate ... Jesus is always meditated and contemplated in an integral manner, in the full divine-human reality as the God-man"] (36-37); 3) its pneumatological aspects ["In Paul, Luke-Acts, and especially John, it is the Spirit who brings us to participate in Jesus ... the Spirit brings us to the whole Christ, the integral Christ"] (37); 4) "its distinction between general and special or unique participation in the mysteries of Jesus" ["The Lord calls us to uniquely personal forms of participation in his mysteries ... the paradigm of unique participation in Jesus' mysteries is, for our principals, the Blessed Virgin Mary"] (39); and 5) a freshness, generativity, and creativity among the principals [the missionary work of all of them; the congregations, apostolic communities, and seminaries they founded; "the renewal of priestly formation and ministry"; "the collaboration with laity and renewal of the laity's call to sanctity"; and their "freshness and creativity in spirituality and theology"] (40-41).

In conclusion, Thompson comments on two special teachings of the French School. "Both touch on the heart of Christology and Trinitarian theology, and both illustrate the meditative knowing by way of loving participation and indwelling that characterizes our School" (41). The first is anéantissement (losing one's life, in the biblical sense)" [a kenosis that "is really a fullness rather than a lack, but such insight is the fruit of a meditative theology"] (41-42). The second is "the fecundity ["the Spirit is fertile"] in the inner Trinity's life outwards, into creation, and most especially in(to) the Incarnation." This later teaching "tries to express the intimate connection between Christology and Pneumatology" (42-43).

Walsh, Eugene Aloysius. "French School of Spirituality" in *New Catholic Encyclopedia*, 13:604-606. Washington, DC: The Catholic University of America Press, 1967.

Walsh identifies the leaders of the French School as Pierre de Bérulle, Charles de Condren, and Jean-Jacques Olier. He notes that, "in addition to these three leaders, two other men developed specific aspects of French School theology into Catholic devotional life: Saint Jean Eudes, the devotion to the Sacred Heart; Saint Louis Marie Grignion de Montfort, true devotion to the Blessed Virgin" (451).

In the brief article, he highlights the following points: general characteristics of the school (451); the Christian mysteries (451); the state of servitude (451); Christ's priestly and victim state (452); and participation in the mysteries (452). The "most characteristic principles and practices of their spiritual teaching" are identified as: "their markedly Christocentric and theocentric concept of religion; their special insight into the doctrine of the Mystical Body in terms of Christ's 'heavenly sacrifice,' His priestly and victim life in heaven and in the Church; and finally, their Christian way of life and prayer as an actual sharing in the mysteries of Christ" (451).

The "French School conceived the way of Christian perfection to be the actual living of the life of Christ, by participating in the mysteries of His life. Christ and His members form one single living victim offered to the glory and the praise of God" (452). "Man cooperates with the Spirit of Jesus, producing in himself the states of Jesus by using his faculties of mind, heart, and will to yield himself to the Spirit of Jesus, to abandon himself to Him, to appropriate the states of Jesus, and to express them in daily living. In this union the person desires to make Christ's life flourish in him at the expense of his own. This is the work of prayer and the practice of virtue" (452).

Walsh, Eugene Aloysius. *The Priesthood in the Writings of the French School: Bérulle, De Condren, Olier.* Washington, DC: The Catholic University of America Press, 1949.

This book is a 135-page extract of Walsh's doctoral dissertation, which comprises three parts: "a study of the original sources of the general teachings of the French School"; "a study of the School's theology of the priesthood and sacrifice of Jesus Christ"; and a consideration of the spiritual consequences of this theology "as applied to the priesthood of the Church" (ix). The second or central part is what is mostly presented in the book since, as Walsh asserts, the doctrine of the French School "served to reform and sanctify the French Secular clergy of the day" (xi). Bérulle's aim "was to bring the clergy not merely to a decent clerical life. He wanted to lift them to a maximum of virtue, to have them live again on earth the holy life of Jesus Christ" (xii).

To achieve their aim, "the masters of the French School unfolded the dogma of the Incarnate Word in all its implications for the spiritual life. The God-man was the central contemplation from which they drew the whole of their spiritual teaching" (xiv). "In language and expression," writes Walsh, "they stand closer to Saint Paul and Saint Augustine and particularly to the Greek Fathers, who were their masters, than to the Scholastics and theologians of their own day" (xv).

A summary of part one of the dissertation, "The General Teaching of the French School," is provided (1-18). The Christian life is "not only hearing and doing the word of Christ … It is more accurately a participating in the 'mysteries' of Christ's life, particularly in those of redemption and sanctification" (2). "The entire Christian life … consists in living on earth the life of Christ, by actually participating in His mysteries and thereby reproducing in ourselves His 'states,' or better, by allowing Christ to live over again His mysteries in us" (12). In their teaching about the mysteries of Christ's life "is found the doctrinal foundation for the sanctifying value of the liturgical life of the Church. For the liturgy is nothing more than the constant representing of the mysteries of Christ so that they can be participated in by the members of His mystical body" (15). "After the sacraments it is chiefly by prayer and the practice of virtue that man personally and willfully participates in the mysteries of Christ" (18).

"The teaching of the French School on the sacrifice and priesthood of Jesus Christ" constitutes part two of the dissertation (19-112). "The central contemplation of the French School from which all their teaching and devotion flows easily and naturally" is their understanding that Christ "remains at the right hand of His Father forever priest and forever victim, and forever the head of His mystical body of which we are the members. Christ, our head, our priest, our victim is now in heaven in the final glory of His priesthood, as the source of all our life" (20).

After considering the sources of the French School's teaching (24-34) [the Epistle to the Hebrews, the tradition of the Greek and Latin Fathers, and the doctrine of Saint Paul], Walsh considers the "heavenly sacrifice" which is Christ under the headings of: "Oblation" (35-45) ["The whole life of Christ is one single sacrifice which began with the Incarnation and continues in heaven"]; "Consummation" (46-68) ["For in the eternal consummation of Christ in the bosom of His Father, in the manifestation of this by the mysteries of the Resurrection and the Ascension, is found the Christ who lives in us to make us participate in the fruits of His Passion and Death"]; and "Heaven, Calvary, the Mass" (69-77) ["Our masters use this language to designate the same sacrifice of Jesus in the three conditions in which we find it, *in facto esse*, as it remains consummated in heaven, *in fieri*, as it happened historically on earth, and in the sacramental order, as it is given to us in the Church"]. Walsh then concludes by considering Christ as "Priest in Heaven" (78-86) ["The entire function of the priesthood of Jesus, then, is to return to God all creation in that very necessary and elementary movement of religion which demands that all which has come from God must go back to Him, as to its principle and end"] and "Victim in Heaven, Victim in the Eucharist" (87-107) ["The disposition of victim that exists in the soul of Jesus, the desire to immolate Himself for the glory of God and for the salvation of souls, is, in the eyes of de Condren and Olier, the highest possible expression of the notion of priesthood and sacrifice"].

A summary of part three of the dissertation, "The Priesthood of the Church," is also provided (113-120). "Father Olier sums up this entire teaching of the French School on the dignity and power and glory of the priesthood when he calls a priest the 'sacrament' of Jesus Christ on earth. The priest is the visible expression of Jesus Christ on earth. He is the efficacious sign of Christ and God. The priest is the 'mystery' of Jesus Christ, just as Christ Himself was the 'mystery' of God on earth, the 'primitive sacrament' of religion" (113).

Wright, Wendy M. "The Salesian and Bérullian Spiritual Traditions" in *Alive for God in Christ Jesus: Proceedings of a Conference on the Contemporary Significance of the French School of Spirituality*, edited by Ronald Bagley et al., 157-167. Buffalo, NY: Saint John Eudes Center, 1995.

Pierre de Bérulle and Francis de Sales, who were both products of Jesuit education, "are considered to be founders of two distinct and 'original spiritual currents,' the Salesian and Bérullian schools of spirituality" (157). Wright suggests "the Salesian current intertwines with the broader context of French spirituality after De Sales' death" (157).

The Salesian spirit, which the author contends is the co-creation of Francis de Sales and Jeanne de Chantal, is presented in six points: 1) a "spirituality embedded in the thought world of Christian humanism" ["affirming the essential goodness and Godward capacity of humanity"]; 2) a spirituality that "emphasizes living between the two wills of God" ["the 'signified will,' that is, the fruits of human discernment" and "'God's good pleasure,' those circumstances, events, and obstacles that are beyond human anticipation and control"]; 3) a spirituality that "emphasizes finding God, practicing the devout life, in the busyness of one's ordinary duties" ["relationships themselves are the vessels that take one to God"]; 4) a "spirituality that emphasizes a holy freedom" ["each person is understood to have freedom of choice in love"]; 5) a heart-centered spirituality ["the entire Salesian universe is imaged as a universe of hearts" and "at its core is the heart of God"]; and 6) a spirituality that has "a preference for the hidden and unnoticed" [Jesus "lives hidden in the heart and love expresses itself ... primarily in the little things"] (158-160).

While distinctive, the two so-called schools share a common historical matrix: "the reforming principles articulated in the Council of Trent"; "a vision of the spiritual life as 'contemplation in action'"; "the vitalization of Christ's body, the church, on all levels"; "engaged in a mission to spread and deepen [God's] love among all God's people"; and "a mystical sensibility that the Christian life was most truly conceived as a profound interior transformation, a ceding of self so that, to quote Saint Paul, 'I no longer live but Christ lives in me'" (160-161).

In comparing the two spiritualities Wright observes that while De Sales embraces "a view that God intended all humankind to be saved," Bérulle's "view of human nature is more guarded, more aware of limitation and impotence in matters salvific" (161). De Sales "perceives that the ontological 'distance' between humankind and God is less profound than the distance envisioned by Bérulle" (162). "If Bérullian spirituality has been characterized as primarily individual and vertical, Salesian spirituality might well be characterized as relational and horizontal" (162). While both masters "assumed that freedom was necessary for growth in God – freedom from inordinate attachments ... Bérulle couples his notion of freedom with that of servitude or even bondage" (162). "Beginning with human experience and analogy is very much De Sales' way ... Bérulle, on the other hand, begins with the grandeur and inaccessibility of God" (164).

Wright concludes her remarks by observing that "these two spiritual currents [and others that provide the broader context] intertwined and mirrored one another during the course of the [seventeenth] century" (164). "It has become commonplace to claim that both Jean Olier and Jean Eudes were influenced by De Sales' teaching in a way that Bérulle himself was not" (165). Vincent de Paul "had a Salesian preference for the marginalized and hidden which manifested itself in his tireless work on behalf of the poor, orphaned, and enslaved" (166). "Jeanne de Chantal's prayer of 'simple remise,' although particularly suited to her religious community, bears a striking resemblance to the teachings of Brother Lawrence of the Resurrection, the Parisian Carmelite lay Brother ... John Baptist de La Salle, clearly a direct disciple of the Bérullian school, met and admired Brother Lawrence as did many other notables in the later part of the century" (167).

Endnotes

1 Yves Krumenacker, *The French School of Spirituality: Mystics, Founders, Movements, and Their Interpreters*, (Paris: Les Editions du Cerf, 1999).

2 Michel Sauvage, "The Gospel Journey of John Baptist de La Salle" in *Sprituality in the Time of John Baptist de La Salle*, edited by Robert C. Berger and translated by Luke Salm (Landover, MD: Lasallian Publications, 1999), pp. 221-246.

3 Sauvage, "The Gospel Journey of John Baptist de La Salle," pp. 222-223.

4 André Rayez, "The Spirituality of Self-Abandonment: Saint John Baptist de La Salle" in *Sprituality in the Time of John Baptist de La Salle*, edited by Robert C. Berger and translated by Philip Smith (Landover, MD: Lasallian Publications, 1999), pp. 133-167.

5 Rayez, "The Spirituality of Self-Abandonment: Saint John Baptist de La Salle," p. 134.

6 Rayez, "The Spirituality of Self-Abandonment: Saint John Baptist de La Salle," p. 133.

7 André Rayez, "Lasallian Studies in the Mid-Twentieth Century" in *Sprituality in the Time of John Baptist de La Salle*, edited by Robert C. Berger and translated by Philip Smith (Landover, MD: Lasallian Publications, 1999), pp. 81-131.

8 Rayez, "Lasallian Studies in the Mid-Twentieth Century," p. 89.

9 Rayez, "Lasallian Studies in the Mid-Twentieth Century," p. 111.

10 Rayez, "Lasallian Studies in the Mid-Twentieth Century," pp. 111-122.

11 Maurice-Auguste Hermans, "Some Spiritual Currents Which Could Have Influenced De La Salle" in *AXIS: Journal of Lasallian Higher Education*, Vol. 4, No. 1 (2013).

12 Hermans, "Some Spiritual Currents Which Could Have Influenced De La Salle," p. 2.

13 Miguel Campos, "Introduction" in *Meditations for the Time of Retreat*, translated by Augustine Loes (Romeoville, IL: Christian Brothers Conference, 1975), pp. 1-44.

14 Campos, "Introduction," p. 5.

15 Campos, "Introduction," p. 6.

16 Cf. *Vincentian Heritage*, Vol. 11, No. 1 (1990), which contains all of the papers from the Conference on "The Age of Gold: The Roots of Our Tradition."

17 Jean-Guy Rodrigue, *Conribution á l'étude des sources des meditations sur les principals festes de l'année. Cahiers lasalliens 47* (Rome: Brothers of the Christian Schools, 1988).

18 Raymond Deville, *The French School of Spirituality*, translated by Agnes Cunningham (Pittsburgh, PA: Duquesne University Press, 1994), p. 171.

19 Krumenacker, *The French School of Spirituality*, p. 514.

20 Cf. Henri Brémond, *A Literary History of Religious Thought in France, Vol. III, The Triumph of Mysticism* (London: Society for Promoting Christian Knowledge, 1936).

21 What is here presented in four paragraphs as the "Introduction" is a translation, in its entirety, of the back jacket of the Krumenacker book.

22 Krumenacker, *The French School of Spirituality*, the heading of Chapter VI.

23 Krumenacker, *The French School of Spirituality*, the preceding paragraph can be found in the original on page 410.

24 Deville, *The French School of Spirituality*, pp. 153-154.

25 Krumenacker, *The French School of Spirituality*, the preceding three paragraphs entitled "Characteristics of the School" can be found in the original on pages 411-412.

26 We return here to the vocabulary and the general schema proposed by Raymond Hostie in *The Life and Death of Religious Orders,* translated

by the Center for Applied Research in the Apostolate (Washington, DC: CARA, 1983).

27 Krumenacker, *The French School of Spirituality*, the preceding three paragraphs can be found in the original on pages 414-415.

28 Krumenacker, *The French School of Spirituality*, the preceding paragraph can be found in the original on page 420.

29 Krumenacker, *The French School of Spirituality*, this entire section on John Baptist de La Salle can be found in Chapter VIII of the original on pages 514-529.

30 The principal works about John Baptist de La Salle are those of Yves Poutet, and particularly his thesis *Le XVII siècle et les origines lasalliennes* (Rennes, 1970); and, about his spirituality, see Michel Sauvage and Miguel Campos, *Announcing the Gospel to the Poor,* translated by Matthew J. O'Connell (Romeoville, IL: 1981) and *AXIS: Journal of Lasallian Higher Education,* Vol. 3, No. 1 (2012) for the two missing chapters of the 1981 English-language translation. A recent biography, of good quality, is that of Yves Poutet, *Saint Jean-Baptiste de La Salle: Un saint du XVII siècle* (Paris, 1992).

31 Jean-Baptiste Blain, *The Life of John Baptist de La Salle: Book One,* translated by Richard Arnandez (Landover, MD: Lasallian Publications, 2000), p.114.

32 *Meditations by John Baptist de La Salle* (Landover, MD: Lasallian Publications, 1994), 62.2.

33 *Meditations by John Baptist de La Salle,* 22.2.

34 *Meditations by John Baptist de La Salle,* 62.3.

35 *Meditations by John Baptist de La Salle,* 54.3.

36 John Baptist de La Salle, *Explanation of the Method of Interior Prayer* (Landover, MD: Lasallian Publications, 1995), pp.110-111.

37 John Baptist de La Salle, *Collection of Various Short Treatises* (Landover, MD: Lasallian Publications, 1993), p.32.

38 *Meditations by John Baptist de La Salle,* 196.3.

39 *Meditations by John Baptist de La Salle,* 86.3.

40 *Meditations by John Baptist de La Salle,* 201.1 & 201.2.

41 *Meditations by John Baptist de La Salle,* 39.3.

42 Poutet, *Le XVII siècle et les origines lasalliennes.*

43 Krumenacker, *The French School of Spirituality,* the preceding three paragraphs can be found in the original on pages 616-618.

Author / Contributors

Yves Krumenacker is a French historian. He mainly studies the religious history of modern France, especially the spirituality of the seventeenth century and Protestantism. He has worked at the Université Jean-Moulin – Lyon III and as a senior member of the Institut Universitaire de France.

Brother William Mann, FSC, who received a Doctor of Ministry degree from Colgate Rochester Divinity School (1990), serves as the president of Saint Mary's University of Minnesota since 2008. He is a former Vicar General of the Brothers of the Christian Schools (2000-2007). Since 1988, he has been a presenter at the Buttimer Institute of Lasallian Studies.

Brother Gerard Rummery, FSC, holds a Doctor of Philosophy degree from Lancaster University. Fluent in French, Spanish, Italian, and German, he served two periods on the staff of the International Lasallian Center in Rome and was twice elected to the General Council of the De La Salle Christian Brothers (1986-1993 and 1993-2000). For many years, he was a presenter in the USA at the Buttimer Institute of Lasallian Studies. Since 2000, he works mainly with educators as a presenter for Lasallian Education Services in Australia.